DODGE CITY

Cowboy Capital...Beautiful Bibulous Babylon...

Queen of the Cowtowns...Wicked Little City...

...the Delectable Burg...

by

Betty Braddock
Jeanie Covalt

KANSAS HERITAGE CENTER

Library of Congress Catalog Number: 82—82026
ISBN 1-882404-03-3
Copyright 1982 by Kansas Heritage Center, Dodge City, Kansas 67801
3rd printing, 1994

Printed by Spearville News, Incorporated, Spearville, Kansas

CONTENTS

FOREWORD

From the early days of our country, Americans have been fascinated with the Old West. Tales told, newspaper accounts, dime novels, movies, and television have all pricked our interest, yet it is these very sources that have established the myths about cowboys, Indians, gunfighters, and cowtowns. When I moved to Dodge City, I was infected with the Western Myth, but during my six years in the community and many hours spent in the Kansas Heritage Center, I began to separate the fact from the myth. I was surprised to learn that the truth is far more exciting than the myth.

This book is important for three reasons. First, Betty Braddock and Jeanie Covalt have separated the myth from reality so we can believe what we read. Second, Dodge City is a unique town and deserves recognition for the legacy it has left America. Third, the book is short and easy to read. It give a brief sketch of but a few of the interesting people and events from the history of Dodge City. We are not burdened with a great deal of unwanted information.

There is one danger in reading this book, however. As you go through the pages, you may read something that pricks your interest and find yourself spending more time than you had planned searching for information on a particular topic. So as you read, beware.

Kansas State University   Dr. Michael Perl

PREFACE

Dodge City was blessed from its beginning with a superabundance of publicity, much of it notorious. The new little frontier town became the darling of metropolitan reporters who enlarged ordinary happenings into outrageous incidents. In that respect Dodge needed no help because ordinary day-by-day life was more uninhibited than in any other place in America.

To study Dodge City or any town, we must realize that towns and cities do not sprout and grow like mushrooms; there must be a need for the services and goods a town can supply. If the needs continue and the town keeps filling those needs, the town grows; if not, the town dies and becomes a ghost town. Dodge City began because soldiers from Fort Dodge and buffalo hunters needed stores, hotels, restaurants and entertainment. There are some very good reasons why the needs were here rather than a few miles away; why a town had to grow in this particular place. There are also some fortunate coincidences that caused the needs to continue, enabling the town to grow and flourish.

We want to thank Noel Ary for his graphic and photographic help without which the book would have been very dull in appearance; and Jennie Burrichter and Mike Perl for their editorial suggestions, encouragement and support.

Jeanie Covalt
Betty Braddock

May, 1982

BUFFALO CITY

Daughter of the Hide Hunters

Dodge City's equal never existed in all the west, not even in the mining camps of the boom days. It was a product of the frontier — of times and conditions that can never exist again.

Robert M. Wright, **Dodge City, The Cowboy Capital**

Dodge City was founded in August, 1872. But, long before that things were happening in the United States that led to the need for a town to be here.

Travel over the Santa Fe Trail, between Missouri, and Santa Fe had been going on for fifty years before Dodge City was founded. The wagons rumbled along right where the town is now — thousands of wagons each year taking merchandise to sell for silver and gold in Santa Fe which then was a part of Mexico. Trail Street was called Santa Fe Trail because it really was the road of this trail.

Fort Dodge was established in 1865 to protect the wagon trains on the Trail from Indians and to furnish supplies to the soldiers who were fighting the Indian wars on the plains. The first buildings were tents, dugouts and sod houses which were used until stone buildings could be finished.

The Fort was a bustling place with much coming and going. Robert M. Wright operated the Sutler Store, a civilian business which sold goods to soldiers, civilians and travelers on the wagon trains. Custer led the 7th Cavalry out of Fort Dodge to the Indian campaigns in Indian Territory. All of the equipment and supplies for the army were shipped to them by heavy freight wagons from Fort Dodge. Indians were frequent visitors, and most of the time camps of tipis were within sight of the Fort. The soldiers looked forward to visits from Satanta, Kicking Bird, Little Raven and others as a relief from the boredom of army life.

Sutler Store, Fort Dodge, 1867

The Indians were dependent on buffalo to provide meat for food and hides for clothing and tipi material. During these early days millions of buffalo roamed the plains. In November, 1872, *The Kansas Commonwealth,* a Topeka newspaper reported:

> The buffaloes are moving south and crossing the Arkansas. Twenty miles west of Dodge an immense herd of the creatures two miles wide and ten miles long were passed by the construction train. It took two hours for the train to get through this herd. Fourteen animals were killed and several calves injured.

Easterners, always looking for something new and exotic from the Wild West, paid good prices for buffalo meat and robes. It was fine meat and made a satisfying meal; also, the robes (hides with the hair left on) made practical, warm coats and blankets.

Hunters swarmed over the area killing the buffalo to sell for a good price. A successful day's hunt might net the hunter a hundred dollars. The same Topeka newspaper article said:

> Every ravine is full of hunters, and camp fires can be seen for miles in every direction. The hides and meat of 1400 buffalo were brought in to town today.[1]

As word spread about the good hunting and about the railroad that would soon reach Western Kansas, men in different parts of the state got the idea of starting businesses near the new railroad tracks and near Fort Dodge to supply the hunters with the necessities for their trade.

George M. Hoover arrived first and opened a saloon — not even in a building, but with only a board laid between two stacks of sod supports. This was in June, 1872, and within a few weeks there were several more saloons, dance halls, restaurants, general merchandise stores, a barbershop, a drug store and a blacksmith shop. At this time there were no trees, not even along the river, so wood for construction had to be hauled by wagons from Hays or other towns; therefore, only a few of the businesses were housed in wooden buildings. The rest were in tents or dugouts.[2]

One saloon, owned by Tom Sherman, was a simple frame building with a canvas roof and a dirt floor.

> "As I was passing by Tom Sherman's bar room
> Tom Sherman's bar room so early one day
> Who should I see but a handsome young cowboy
> Stretched out on a blanket and all pale and gray."[3]

This is one version of "The Cowboy's Lament," a song which also is known as "Beat the Drum Slowly" and "Streets of Laredo." In the Tom Sherman version, the young cowboy "got shot in the breast by a Dodge City gambler."

In August, two months after Hoover had opened the first business, the men of the town and a few officers from Fort Dodge met to organize a real town which they called Buffalo City. Since the name Buffalo had been chosen by another town and could not be used again in Kansas, the new little city became Dodge City. Perhaps this name was suggested because Colonel Richard I. Dodge, Commandant at Fort Dodge, was one of the Town Company members or perhaps because the town was near Fort Dodge.

In September the first train arrived on the newly laid tracks. Already buffalo hides were stacked high waiting to be shipped to the East.

> *Hardly had the railroad reached there before business began; and such a business! Dozens of cars a day were loaded with hides and meat, and dozens of carloads of grain, flour and provisions arrived each day. The streets of Dodge were lined with wagons bringing in hides and meat and getting supplies from early morning to late at night.[4]*

Dodge City was now a full-fledged chartered town, wide open and ready for business. As one old-timer said, "Dodge warn't no nickel and dime town."

This explains four of the reasons a town had to be started in this place and why it would grow.

First, the Santa Fe Trail with thousands of wagons traveling between Missouri and Santa Fe caused a need for forts to be built for protection of the travelers.

Second, Fort Dodge was established to protect the wagon trains and as a supply depot for the armies on the southern plains.

Third, the big business of buffalo hunting caused a need for stores to sell supplies and to buy the hides and meat.

Fourth, the coming of the railroad allowed provisions to be brought to the Dodge City stores as well as to haul out the goods that Dodge Citians wanted to sell. The railroad boosted the population by bringing new people who worked for the rail company. It also made Dodge City the center of a large trade area.

Buffalo Hunting

Chas. Rath & Co. hide yard alongside the railroad, where hides were unloaded, stretched, dried and baled for shipment to tanneries.

The buffalo killing rampage was launched when a new tanning process was discovered in Germany for turning the buffalo hides into usable leather. An English company ordered 500 hides from a Fort Leavenworth dealer. A Pennsylvania tanner ordered 2,000 hides at $3.50 each. The boom was on!

Legislatures in the western states passed laws to protect the buffalo from massive slaughter; but these laws could not be enforced. General Phil Sheridan appeared before the Texas legislature and said:

> These men (hunters) have done more in the last two years and will do more in the next, to settle the vexed Indian opposition than the entire regular Army has done in thirty years. They are destroying the Indian's commissary . . . For the sake of peace, let them kill, skin and sell until the buffalos are exterminated.[5]

The professional buffalo hunters were a lusty lot, hardened to weather and danger. They had to be to take the hard, bloody work, the storms, the bad water and the Indian attacks. A hunting outfit included one or more hunters, several skinners and enough wagons to carry the equipment.

The hunter rode out early in the morning to spot a herd, crawled to within about 300 yards, set up rest sticks to level the rifle and started shooting. Some hunters favored Sharps rifles while other popular guns were Remingtons, Ballards and Springfields, all single shot. At that time repeating rifles did not have strong enough breech mechanisms to stand the heavy powder charges needed to kill a buffalo. Each hunter carried a reloading outfit, bullet molds and other necessary items to load ammunition.[6]

When the hunt was over the skinners rode out to begin their grisly work. A professional skinner took pride in seeing that the hides he peeled were free of knife gashes. He used butcher knives which he owned by the case, and carried a sharpening steel on his belt.

Back in camp the skinner threw the hides on the ground, flesh side up, cut small holes around the outside edges, and drove wooden pegs through the holes into the ground thus stretching the hide into a uniform shape. A dried bull hide weighed 50 pounds or more, a cow hide 20 pounds. Prime hides were cured for a longer time. Uncured hides were called "green," the finished products, "flint" hides. The efficient outfits sprinkled poison over the hides to kill insects. Untreated hides might be partially eaten by the insects and could not be sold.[7]

Some outfits also cured and sold the meat at prices ranging from 4¢ to 6¢ a pound. Smoked buffalo tongues, always a delicacy, brought 20¢ to 50¢ each and were shipped east to the fine restaurants. A few hunters took only the tongues.

By 1879 the wholesale slaughter had eliminated the great southern herd. Some hunters went north, but by 1883 the northern herd had met the same fate.

Dodge was the home base for many interesting men who engaged in buffalo hunting — Prairie Dog Dave Morrow who killed a white buffalo, Mysterious Dave Mather, Wyatt Earp, the Masterson brothers and others. Mention is made here of two men especially: Charles Rath because his life on the plains was so remarkable; and George W. Reighard because he left a vivid description of the business of buffalo hunting.

George W. Reighard

After serving as a Union soldier in the Civil War George Reighard came west to Hays in 1867 to enter the government freighting service between there and Fort Dodge. After two years he acquired freighting outfits of his own and made his headquarters at Fort Dodge.

In 1930 Mr. Reighard was interviewed by A. B. MacDonald of the *Kansas City Star* and the following excerpts in the first person graphically tell the story of his experiences in the high plains:

I went west in 1867, and for several years drove a government team in the reserve train for General Custer and the 7th Cavalry, our route being from Ft. Hays to Ft. Dodge, on the Arkansas river, and on south to Ft. Supply in Texas [Oklahoma], and back again. This was through the heart of buffalo country. On those long drives I was always deeply interested in watching the buffalo herds come in the springtime, following the northward moving sun and the upspringing grass.

As soon as the grass, which had been brown all winter, began to take on a greenish tinge, the first buffaloes would appear from the south, beyond the Arkansas singly and in groups of twos and threes, the advance skirmishers of the main herd. Then we would have fresh buffalo meat. As the grass grew, and the prairie greened, the buffaloes came thicker and thicker until the whole earth, as far as the eye could see, was covered with them, moving slowly, in a general northerly direction, grazing as they went.

I cannot blame a youngster today for smiling in a cynical way when I tell him that this northward drifting herd had a frontal width of 100 and often 200 miles, but it had. I stood on top of Mt. Jesus, south of Ft. Dodge, and saw the whole country, clear off to where sky and earth merged in a purplish haze, covered with one mass of buffaloes. To the eastward, away to the north and the west and south, one herd of buffaloes, and I saw that, not only in one year, but each spring for years.

I do not mean that the prairie was black with them. The buffalo was not black, anyway, although many writers have said he was. Audubon, the bird man, who knew colors as well as anyone, and knew the buffalo, too, described his color as "between a dark umber and liver-shining brown." I would call it a kind of yellowish brown. I have read after many writers who described a herd as "Blackening the plains." They never herded that closely together. A grazing herd, undisturbed, would be divided into small groups, each group close together, and there could be ordinarily, about twenty-five or thirty buffaloes to the acre. They drifted along, about as closely together as cattle cluster when grazing loosely on the range. But, looking at a buffalo herd from a knoll or hill, it seemed to be almost a solid mass, with the green sod showing only here and there, between groups.

In One Herd For 175 Miles
On one of our trips, in the spring, from Ft. Hays southward, we met the advancing herd at

Pawnee, fifty miles south of Ft. Hays, and from there, clear on to Ft. Supply, 175 miles, we traveled through a continuous mass of buffaloes grazing slowly northward. Often we would be stopped by a group of a few hundred that was so compact it blocked the way and we would wait until it drifted past and a lane opened ahead of us.

I have read of a Russian ice breaking steamer battling its way through the ice floes to reach the survivors of Nobile's airship, how it would nose this way and that along the lanes between the floating ice cakes. In much the same manner we navigated through that vast drifting herd of buffaloes.

In those days buffaloes were not so suspicious of man as they became later, and this herd was too busy feeding to bother us or be frightened by us. They would lift their shaggy heads, gaze curiously at us for a moment and then go on feeding. But at one place the herd became frightened at something and stampeded right through our train, which consisted of thirty wagons, each drawn by six mules. The herd came with such force that it overturned six of the heavily loaded wagons.

I have ridden on trains on the Kansas Pacific railroad west of Ft. Hays that were stopped for hours by buffaloes streaming across the track ahead. When that road was first built out across buffalo land, the engineers, meeting herds like that, tried to force their trains through them, but not even a locomotive could open a way, and after several engines had been shunted off the rails by the bodies of buffaloes piling up beneath the wheels, the engineers abandoned the attempt to head off a moving buffalo herd.

I have often listened to the noise of a buffalo herd on the march across the prairie, the thousands of hoofs on the hard sod, with their dewclaws rattling, sounding like the pounding and clattering of a freight train crossing a high, long wooden bridge. That sound of buffaloes on the march could be heard a mile and more away like the toll of distant thunder. In the breeding season of the buffalo I have often laid under a wagon or by a camp fire out on the plains and heard the bellowing of the bulls, like a mighty roar, all through the night, even when the herd was out of sight, more than a mile distant.

An Indian Belief

All Indians I ever talked with about it believed that buffaloes were not born as other animals, but were created by the Great Spirit each spring in a mammoth cave beneath the earth somewhere down south, beyond the Brazos, the Red and Rio Grande rivers, and that when the grass began to turn green they issued in millions from the cave's mouth, like swarming bees, to drift up north and feed the Indians. I asked an old Indian once:

"You've seen buffalo calves born on the prairie, and seen the calves with the herds — how about that?"

"Oh, yes," he answered, "A few were born on the prairie, but not enough could be born to make up so many, plentiful as the grass blades."

Indians Preferred Bow and Arrow

In 1872, when I went down into the Texas Panhandle with a buffalo hunting outfit, it was estimated the southern herd numbered 3 million head. By that time buffalo hunting had been developed into an exact science. Until the railroads, the breech-loading rifles and the big demand for hides came in together, nearly all the buffalo robes were supplied by Indians and a few whites who hunted on horseback. Even then the favorite weapon of the Indian was the bow and arrow. He had practiced with them since he was big enough to lift a bow, and was more accurate with them than with a rifle. I have seen an Indian drive an arrow into a buffalo clean up to the feather, but that could only be done when the head did not strike a bone.

Two thicknesses of flint-dry buffalo hide is bullet proof. Even a "big fifty" Sharps' rifle bullet would not penetrate it. I have seen an Indian drive an arrow through one thickness of such a hide, but that had to be done at short range. An arrow could be shot 200 yards, but it lost most of its power after fifty yards.

But there was scarcely any danger at all from buffaloes in still hunting, and it was buffalo butchery by wholesale. One still hunter, with two high-powered breech-loaders, plenty of cartridges and a good hiding place behind a clump of brush or weeds, within good range of a grazing or resting herd, could kill one a minute so long as the herd stood for it. Charley Hart killed ninety buffaloes in an hour and a half, exactly one a minute.

Killed Without Stampeding Herds

In 1872 I organized my own outfit and went south from Ft. Dodge to shoot buffaloes for their hides. I furnished the team and wagon and did the killing. Jim Whalen, Tom Rooney and Zeke Ford furnished the supplies and did the skinning and stretching and cooking. They got half the hides and I the other half. I had two big .50 Sharps rifles with telescopic sights, using a shell three and one-half inches long, with 110 grains of powder. Those guns would kill a buffalo as far away as you could see it, if the bullet hit the right spot.

We had flour, coffee, sugar, salt, blankets, four 10-gallon kegs for water, a dutch oven, two frying pans, a big tin coffee pot, a camp kettle, bread pan, tin cups and plates, but no table knives, forks or spoons. We used our skinning and ripping knives for carving and "fingers were made before forks" anyhow. We had four butcher steels and a grindstone for sharpening knives, and that just about completed our outfit. Our diet was mostly buffalo meat, fried, stewed or raw — anyway — and, as there was plenty of that, we saved the expense and worry of toting a lot of provisions around.

We kept moving the camp as the herd moved, often staying a week in a camp. Each morning I would either ride out or walk, depending on how far away the herd was. Usually I went to the top of some rise to spy out the herd, and I could creep and crawl, taking advantage of gullies and ridges, to sneak up to within good range. Between 200 and 350 yards was all right, the closer the better. I would choose my spot, behind some natural screen, a soap-weed, cactus, sagebrush, or the like, would lie flat on my stomach, get my guns ready, spread a lot of cartridges out on the ground, adjust the gun sights, and be ready to shoot. Usually I carried a gun rest made from a tree crotch which I would stick in the ground to rest the gun barrel upon.

It required a great deal of strategy born of experience to handle a buffalo "stand" so as to kill as many as possible before the herd became frightened and stampeded. Usually the herd group selected for a stand would be grazing slowly, unsuspicious of danger. Each group always had a leader. The general belief is that the leader was an old bull; it is so recorded in nearly all books I have read about it. But that was not so. The leader was the oldest cow in the group, so the first move of the still-hunter would be to drop her. If aimed true the bullet would pierce her lungs. She would make a startled movement, a sort of little leap forward, looking around, the blood gushing from her nostrils. The animals near her, hearing the report of the gun, would look to her, with probably an idea of running if she would lead the way, but without initiative to start a stampede; they would see her standing still and would resume their grazing. The wounded cow would wabble, weakly, then stagger forward and fall.

Meantime, I would have jammed another shell in the breech and watching the herd carefully, I would note any movement on the part of any buffalo to take flight and start off, and that one would be the next victim. It would begin bleeding, lurching unsteadily, and would fall. Several would walk up and sniff at the two on the ground. They would throw up their heads and bawl, one or two might start off, and then I must drop them. Sometimes the whole herd would start. Then I must shoot quickly, dropping the leaders, which would turn the others back. The whole idea was to keep the herd milling, round and round, in one restricted spot, shooting those on the outskirts that tried to move away.

Fired Until Gun Was Hot

While this was going on the only strange thing the buffaloes could see was a little puff of white smoke now and then from a distant bush or rock. This was not alarming, usually, and they would generally stay, milling and bawling, bewildered, until most of them were shot.

The time I made my biggest kill I lay on a slight ridge, behind a tuft of weeds, 100 yards from a bunch of a thousand buffaloes that had come a long distance to a creek, had drunk their fill and then strolled out upon the prairie to rest, some to lie down. I followed the tactics I have described. After I had killed about twenty five my gun barrel became hot and began to expand. A bullet from an overheated gun does not go straight, it wabbles, so I put that gun aside and took the other. By the time that became hot the other had cooled, but then the powder smoke in front of me was so thick I could not see through it; there was not a breath of wind to carry it away, and I had to crawl backward, dragging my two guns, and work around to another position on the ridge, from which I killed fifty-four more. In one and one-half hours I had fired 91 shots, as a count of the empty shells showed afterward, and had killed 79 buffaloes, and we figured that they all lay within an area of about two acres of ground. My right hand and arm were so sore from working the gun that I was not sorry to see the remaining buffaloes start off on a brisk run that soon put them beyond my range. I could then get to my feet and stretch.

Pity? No, I did not feel it. It was business with me. I had my money invested in that outfit; if I did not butcher the buffaloes there were many other hunting outfits all around me that would, so I killed all I could. I have often heard of still hunters killing one hundred and more in one stand. On that trip I killed a few more than 3,000 buffaloes in one month, which was an average of about 100 a day.

Cured the Hides On the Ground

While the still hunter was shooting buffaloes his skinners were hidden nearby waiting for the killing to end. Then they came out and stripped the hides off the carcasses while they were yet warm. The professional skinner was an expert in his line and could rip the hide off a buffalo with amazing swiftness. His tools were a ripping knife, sharp-pointed and keen as a razor blade; a skinning knife, sharp, but with a more blunted point, and a butcher's steel — all dangling in scabbards from his belt.

The hide was spread out on the grass, hair side down, and left to cure and dry in the sun. In later years, when buffaloes were scarce and hides brought a higher price, the skins were often pegged out on the ground; that is, slits would be cut in the edges all around and sharpened pegs driven through into the ground to hold the hide stretched taut until it dried. But in those early days, when dry hides brought less than a dollar in the field, we simply laid them out to dry. When the hides were dry enough they were folded once, down the middle — the hair inside — and piled into stacks.

A few hunters had their own wagons and hauled their hides to the railroad, but the majority stacked them up in piles to await the coming of the hide buyers. In the early 70's, when we were killing off the southern herd, the whole hide business was systematized, and in Dodge City, Fort Worth and other towns were companies of hide dealers who had buyers on horseback in the field riding from camp to camp, and fleets of heavy freight wagons to haul the hides to the railroad, 100 to 200 miles away. A buyer would come to our camp, pay us for the hides we had, and later the wagons would come and pick them up.

In the early 70's we did not think we were exterminating the buffalo herds. There were 3 million buffaloes there then, enough, we thought, with the natural increase to supply the market for a hundred years to come. It was natural for us to think that, the herds were so large. In later years I saw 10,000 cattle in one round-up, and it wasn't a drop in the bucket compared with a buffalo herd I saw on those very same plains in 1872. You could have put those 10,000 cattle into the buffalo herd and lost them. And yet that vast buffalo herd had become almost extinct in four years. By the spring of 1876 only about 10,000 buffaloes remained, and they had fled from the hunters and were scattered in small bands off toward the Pecos country. The last of the southern herd, about 200 head, were killed off in 1887 by a party led by Lee Howard. Buffaloes were so scarce then that Howard sold the bull heads for mounting for $50 apiece and robes for $20.

Charles Rath

Charles Rath was an itchy-footed frontiersman who left his parent's comfortable home in Ohio in the early 1850's to come to the Kansas Territory. He went first to Bent's Fort (east of present day LaJunta, Colorado) where the mountain men gathered to sell their furs and to trade with Indians. Charles worked there in the commissary for a while then went out on his own as an independent trader among the Cheyenne Indians.

When he was 24 he married a Cheyenne woman, Roadmaker, who may have been a sister of William Bent's wife, Owl Woman. Roadmaker must have been several years older than Charles because she had been married at least twice and had four children. Her first husband, Kit Carson, came home one day from a hunting trip and found all of his belongings thrown out of the tipi. This was the Cheyenne way of divorce. Her name did not mean that she made roads, but that she was very bossy and "laid down the law." Roadmaker and Charles had one child, Cheyenne Belle. The little family moved to near Fort Zarah on Walnut Creek where Charles operated a trading post and stage stop. One day Roadmaker's clan was camped near the post; when they left, she and Belle went with them and never returned.

Charles Rath

Charles Rath sits atop buffalo hides waiting shipment in the Rath & Wright yards at Dodge City.

Alone now, Rath continued his work as a trader and also went into the freighting business, traveling over Central and Western Kansas and into the Oklahoma and Texas Panhandle areas. He learned to speak the languages of most of the Plains tribes, his soft voice being especially adapted to the fluid Cheyenne speech. The German language. he learned as a boy at home, made the guttural Kiowa tongue easier. Charles was admired and respected by the Indians and mediated disputes between them and white men on different occasions. Recent evidence found in correspondence from officers at Fort Dodge to the Department of the Army shows that Rath was suspected of trading whiskey and contraband guns and ammunition to the Indians.[8]

By 1870 Rath was at his prime — mature, successful and increasingly wealthy. He was strong and healthy, well built and agile, a very good horseman. He could be described as handsome with a high broad forehead, black hair, light blue-gray eyes, fair skin, a frontiersman's black moustache and a prominent dimple in his left cheek. He ordered his rich brown suits and white shirts custom-made in New York City and wore expensive custom-made boots.

As a wealthy businessman he returned to Ohio to visit his parents, and while there became reacquainted with a neighbor, nineteen year old Caroline (Carrie) Markley who had just graduated from college. She was a society girl, passionately fond of dancing, expensive clothes and lavish jewelry.

Carrie set her sights on this romantic adventurer from the West. Charles, who had not learned about bossy women from his experience with Roadmaker, was easy prey. They were married before Charles returned to Kansas. They lived for a time in Topeka before moving, in 1872, to the brand new town Dodge City where Charles went into the mercantile business with Robert M. Wright and A. J. Anthony.

Charles Rath & Company was the biggest and most profitable business in Dodge. The store sold all kinds of outfitting goods to the townspeople and buffalo hunters — groceries, blankets, liquors, ropes, knives, clothing, guns and ammunition as well as buying and trading for buffalo hides and meat. The first year in business they shipped over 200,000 buffalo hides east to be tanned, as well as two hundred railroad cars of cured and smoked hindquarters of buffalo meat and two cars of smoked buffalo tongues.

Wright ran the store in Dodge while Rath traveled over the Southwest establishing posts where he bought or traded for hides. Being a hunter, he traveled with twelve wagons pulled by mule teams and twenty-one men who did the butchering and skinning of the animals he killed. Once on the Canadian River Rath killed 103 buffaloes from one stand, which means he shot from one place without moving about.

After five years Charles sold his part of the Dodge City store to spend all of his time attending to the outposts. He established stores in Texas at Fort Griffin, Mobeetie and Fort Elliott. Rath and Wright formed a partnership with Lee and Reynolds, stage line owners, to establish yet another "buffalo town" in Texas. Charles Rath, with a compass swinging from his saddle horn, led a caravan south from Dodge to the Double Mountains (near present Hamlin, Texas) where in 1877 they built Rath City, sometimes called Reynold's City. Slam-bam buildings were thrown together with adobe, sod, buffalo skins and cedar pickets. The largest structure was Rath's Store which provided a full line of merchandise and services for the frontiersman including a Chinese laundry run by Charlie Sing. Rath City also had a blacksmith shop, wagon yard and barber shop. When the saloon and dance hall with girls imported from Dodge City was built, the town was complete. A million dollars worth of hides passed through Rath City, but the venture lasted for only two years.

To keep these far-flung businesses operating and productive Charles had to be gone from home for months at a time. His wife and two children tried living at Fort Griffin, but Carrie did not like the rough life so she and the children moved back to Dodge City. When Charles found time to come home, Carrie scolded him for being gone so long; he could not seem to please her when he was home; then when it was time for him to leave she scolded again. According to Ham Bell, in the fall of 1885, "Charley rode into town stayed a few minutes and rode right back out again." Several weeks later Carrie went to Mr. Bell and begged him to find Charles and ask him to come back to her. She said Charles had told her he was riding out, leaving her everything he had in town and never coming back. Mr. Bell replied, "Knowing Charley Rath as I do, I doubt that he will be coming back, not after telling you he wasn't. You take a good man like Charley, with all the patience in the world, and when he does once kick the traces, he'll be hard to line up again. No, I can't help you there."

Charles sued for divorce in Mobeetie, Texas. Not long after this he married Emma Nesper, a young Philadelphia woman who was visiting in Mobeetie. They had one son, Morris Rath, who became a major league baseball player. After ten years Emma returned to a more social life in Philadelphia. Carrie was married to Thomas Bainbridge, a Dodge City railroad man. He was killed a few years later in a train accident. Charles' and Carrie's children, Robert and Bertha, both married and spent their lives in Dodge City, but neither had children.

Cheyenne Belle and her mother Roadmaker had spent the years after leaving Rath's place on Walnut Creek, with the Cheyennes near Geary, Oklahoma. Belle was thirteen when, alone and hiding in a ravine after an Indian battle, she was picked up by soldiers and taken to the Darlington Indian School. She became one of the most able Cheyenne women and was interpreter for General Phil Sheridan. Belle was married twice and had six children three of whom attended Carlisle Indian Institute. Her son, Mike Belanti, played short-stop for the Cincinnati Reds. After Belle's first child was born, she and her husband, Mike Belanti, took the baby to Mobeetie to visit Charles. Mike had insisted after their marriage that Belle write to her father and get reacquainted. Charles was delighted to see his daughter again and her husband and the new baby. He gave her his special buggy with seats that reclined to make a bed, so she would be comfortable on her way home. His horse herd of forty-four animals was driven in so Mike and Belle could select a team for the buggy. The town dressmakers were busy sewing a new wardrobe for Belle. Charles gave her $250 as a going away present as well as a gift for Roadmaker. Belle visited her father once more at Mobeetie, but Carrie was present also and Belle sensed that she was unwelcome. Belle died in 1939 and is buried at Geary, Oklahoma.

Charles Rath's fortune declined with the vanishing frontier. One by one his resources slipped away. The buffalo trade was over. With the expansion of the railroads, long freight hauling was all but over. Some years earlier Charles had given his brother land near Osage City, Kansas, which was thought to be rich with coal. He moved back to Osage City to help with the coal mine, but it did not produce. He bought a ticket to Trinidad, Colorado, hoping he would be able to collect money from an old debt with which he could travel on to Los Angeles to live with his sister. The person who owed him the money no longer lived in Trinidad, so in desperation he wired his sister, Louisa, for money.

While waiting to hear from her, Charles ground out music on a downtown street with a borrowed hand-organ to get enough money for food.

Charles Rath was 66 years old when he died at Louisa's home in 1902. He is buried in California.[9]

CATTLE TOWN

Buffalo hunting, one of the reasons for the founding of Dodge City, had hardly begun before it was over. The millions of buffalo were being depleted rapidly by wholesale slaughter. In order to survive Dodge would need another source of income. Once again, events taking place in other parts of the country provided that source.

After the Civil War conditions in Texas were ripe for the cattle industry to develop. Men came home from fighting to ranches that has been allowed to run down for the want of labor. The old way of life was gone; new industries and jobs were needed. The Texans saw a possible answer to their problems in the wild native Longhorns which were running free, to be had for the taking. If the cattle could be moved to population centers north and east of the Mississippi, where a meat shortage existed because of the war, they could be sold for badly needed hard cash.

Ranchers in south Texas began rounding up the Longhorns to sell to eastern buyers; but transporting the cattle to the cities was the big problem. No railroads had been built to where the cattle were, and the animals could not be driven all the way to market. They would lose too much weight and be tougher than usual. The solution was to walk the cattle to the nearest railroad shipping point, usually in Kansas, and let them ride the rest of the way.

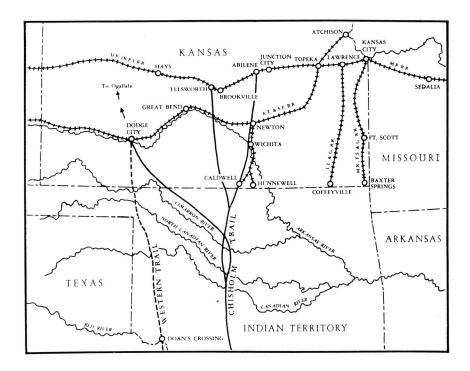

The most famous cattle trail, the Chisholm, began in south Texas and ended at Abilene, Kansas. As eastern and central Kansas became more thickly populated the farmers resented the Texans using their land as open range and ruining the crops. They also feared the "Texas Fever," a disease, caused by a tick carried by the Longhorns, which killed the local cattle. So, the farmers put up fences to keep out the foreign herds. Quarantine laws were passed by the Kansas legislature, and sometimes enforced, that prohibited Texas cattle from moving through certain parts of Kansas. This caused the Chisholm Trail to be discontinued, and cattlemen began using the Western Trail from south Texas to Dodge City, where the Texas trade was welcomed eagerly.

Texas Longhorns in Dodge City, *Leslies,* July 27, 1878

On the trail the hardy Longhorns grazed for food and spaced themselves by instinct as they moved along about 12 miles a day. A steer could be driven from the starting point in Texas to Dodge for about 75 cents. The fifteen or so men employed for the drive were each paid thirty to forty dollars a month; so by the time they reached Dodge $90 or more jingled in their pockets and they were ready to spend it all on a good time.

The first herds reached Dodge City in 1875 and the drives increased until the number of cattle peaked at half a million for one year. 1877 was the first really big cattle year.

Cattle men and cattle dealers are beginning to come in and are selecting their hotel quarters for the summer. They come to stay, to participate in the largest cattle drives ever brought from Texas . . . Thousands of cattle are already on hand with thousands to follow.

Ford County Globe
May 14, 1880

The Santa Fe railroad company built a large new stockyard and Robert Wright sent agents down the trail to assure the drovers that Dodge was ready and waiting for them. Storekeepers bought new merchandise to meet the needs and desires of the cattlemen and cowboys rather than buffalo hunters. Saloon keepers gave their places of business such Texas pleasing names as Nueces, Alamo and Lone Star. In 1877 the first herd from the Red River reached Dodge on May 12.

> In this delectable city of the plains the winter of discontent is made glorious by the return of the cattle trade . . . This cattle village and far-famed wicked city is decked in gorgeous attire in preparation for the long horn . . . Like the sweet harbinger of spring the boot black came . . . Next the barber with his lather and shave. Too, with all that go to make up the busy throng of life's fitful fever, come the Mary Magdalenes, selling their souls to whoever will buy. There is high, low, jack and the game all adding to the great expectation . . . The merchant and the hardware dealer has fitted his store and renovated his palace. There are goods in profusion in warehouses and on shelves . . . There is great ado, for soon the vast plains will be coverd with the long horns.
>
> **Dodge City Times, May 4, 1878**

Robert Wright's store advertised "the largest and fullest line of Groceries and Tobacco west of Kansas City. Everything from a paper of pins to a portable house, groceries, provisions for your camp, ranch or farm; clothing, hats, boots, shoes, underclothing, overalls, Studebaker wagons, Texas saddles, rifles, carbines, pistols, festive Bowie knives, building hardware. Profits $75,000 a year."

Morphy, the editor of the *Globe,* described the Wright store:

> Those gentlemen do an immense business and make a specialty to cater to the Texas trade. The jingling spur, the carved ivory-handled Colt, or the suit of velveteen, and the many, many other Texas necessaries, you will find by the gross or cord. An upstairs room thirty by seventy-five feet, is devoted entirely to clothing and saddlery . . . The house also does a banking business . . . will accomodate you with five dollars or five thousand, as the case may be . . . their sales average a thousand dollars a day, Sundays not excepted.[1]

Wright said it was a common practice to send shipments of $50,000 to banks in Leavenworth for deposit because Dodge had no bank. Most nationalities could be accomodated in the store. Wright could understand and be understood in most Indian languages; Mr. Isaacson spoke French, while Sam Samuels had mastered Spanish, German, Russian and Hebrew.

Merchants and saloon-keepers knew the trail hands expected to have a good time when they reached town; and were ready to provide the right ingredients. The saloons ranged from one-room shanties with dirt floors to long wooden buildings with painted interiors, ornately carved mahogany bars, mirrors and paintings. These frontier saloons offered more than rot gut and snake head whiskies. Fine liqueurs, brandies, and the latest mixed drinks could be had. Ice usually was available so that beer could be served cold. Cowtown drinking was not primitive. The Old House Saloon even advertised anchovies and Russian caviar on its cold lunch menu.[2]

> A pair of expensive oil paintings and a handsome buffalo head were installed in the Long Branch saloon. It is fitted up in elegant style in anticipation of the Texas

cattle trade . . . The Long Branch presents a brilliant appearance by gas light. The walls are handsomely decorated, papered, and in the glare of the dazzling light the spectacle is alluring. The favorite resort is thronged day and night by liquidators, pasteboard manipulators, stock speculators . . .

Dodge City Times, May 22, 1880

There is seldom witnessed in any civilized town or country such a scene as transpired at the Long Branch last Saturday evening resulting in the killing of Levi Richardson, a well known freighter of this city, by a gambler named Frank Loving . . . Richardson was a man who had lived for several years on the frontier, and though well liked, had cultivated habits of bold and daring, which are likely to get a man in trouble . . . He was a hard working, industrious man, but young, strong and reckless. Loving is known to the patrons of the Long Branch as Cock-Eyed Frank, one of his optics bearing in a northeast direction to the other. Cock-Eyed Frank is 25 years old, a gambler by profession of the cool and desperate order.

Ford County Globe, April 8, 1879

A party of eight men had been making some demonstrations across the dead line . . . (The dead line referred to the railroad tracks. North of the tracks were respectable saloons and businesses where gunplay and carrying weapons were discouraged by the police. South of the tracks little effort was made to enforce the ordinance against carrying weapons unless actual fighting broke out or a complaint was made.) On this particular evening the police undertook to disarm a squad of cowboys who had neglected to lay aside their sixshooters. The cowboys protested and war was declared.

Ford County Globe, June 1879

After some rough and tumble fighting with the officers, probably Wyatt Earp and Jim Masterson, the cowboys fled. During these years the law enforcement lists include the Masterson brothers, Ed, Bat and Jim, Wyatt Earp, Bill Tilghman, Mysterious Dave Mather and Pat Sughrue. The shootings never were as many or as frequent as shown in books or on television; but had more publicity because they happened in Dodge.

Not all of the entertainment centered around the saloons and dance halls. The Reynolds Stage Line kept a pet buffalo.

Yesterday the buffalo observed the Simon Comedy Company's Hussar band parading the streets and took exception, and with head down and tail up charged the band. The music ceased and the band did some excellent running. It was the worst broke up parade you ever saw.

Globe Livestock Journal, February 23, 1886

On last Tuesday morning the champion prize fight was indulged in by Messrs. Nelson Whitman and the noted Red Hanley, familiarly known as "the Red Bird from the South." . . . During the forty-second round Red implored the referee to take Nelson off for a little while till he could have time to put his right eye back where it belonged, set his jaw and have the ragged edge trimmed off his ears . . . About the sixty-first round Red squealed unmistakable, and Whitman was declared winner.

Dodge City Times, June 16, 1877

The children of Dodge City gathered at Kelley's Opera House Christmas Eve. After singing and recitations the highlight of the celebration came at last when "Old Santa," clothed in the conventional Arctic garb . . . made glad the hearts of the children by informing them, in song, that he had presents for one and all, both great and small.

Ford County Globe, January 1883

By 1885 the end of the cattle trail was evident. Farmers were fencing their lands; railroads had been extended closer to the cattle; and most importantly, the quarantine law was enforced.

There are silent but irresistible forces at work to regenerate Dodge City . . . rapid settlement of the country south and southwest of Dodge, have destroyed that place as a cattle town. The cowboy must go and with him will go the gamblers, the courtesans, the desperadoes and the saloons.

Topeka Capital, 1885

Dodge City's cattle era lasted only ten years, 1875-1885, but these were the years that determined her reputation and world-wide fame. Now it was time for the Queen of the Cowtowns to settle down as a farming community and trade center.

Olé!

Before settling down to an ordinary small-town existence, Dodge had to have one last, glorious, outrageous hoorah. What would be more outrageous than a bullfight? Former mayor, A. B. Webster proposed the idea of a genuine Mexican bullfight to celebrate the Fourth of July and to bring Dodge again to national acclaim and popularity. Webster later said he did not know how he happened to think of the idea, but as soon as he had it he proceeded to examine the statute books, and finding no law against it pushed the matter for all it was worth.

Most of the business men thought Webster's idea a good one. It would rescue businesses which were suffering from a slowing down of the cattle trade. Also, Dodge had always been a sporting town and a bullfight certainly would be different from the usual parade, races, prize fights and hose-cart team competition. However,

A number of so-called good and moral people of the city have attempted to convey the impression . . . that there will be no bull fight . . . The reports were started by the same class of fanatical agitators who are eternally opposing every enterprise calculated to advertise Dodge and promote its growth and prosperity . . . It is the same class of men who have for years done nothing but howl and kick and at the same time grow wealthy and fat.

Dodge City Democrat, June 28, 1884

In only two days Webster collected $10,000 from the merchants to pay for the festivities. The investors formed the Dodge City Driving Park and Fair Association and elected Ham Bell as president and Webster as general manager. Webster started immediately making arrangements. He contacted W. K. Moore, an attorney in Mexico, who would secure the matadors. D. W. "Doc" Barton who had driven the first trail herd to Dodge, agreed to scout the ranges and select the most ferocious Longhorn bulls. The Association bought forty acres of land at the west edge of the city. They put up high wooden fences, planted trees, built corrals, chutes, a half-mile racetrack and an amphitheater that would seat 2,500 spectators — all in less than two months.

The news stories began. Reporters from New York, Chicago, St. Louis, San Franciso, Denver and a dozen country newspapers booked rooms in the local hotels. The Santa Fe railroad announced it would run excursion trains from the East and the West to bring spectators to the Dodge City bullfight. Groups concerned with the prevention of cruelty to animals protested to the governor. There were rumors that state authorities would stop the fight; however, Governor Glick sent a letter to the Dodge City officials saying that he would like to attend if the fight were held two days earlier. It was claimed that Webster received a telegram from the United States Attorney saying that bullfighting was against the law in the United States, to which the ex-mayor retorted, "Hell! Dodge City ain't in the United States."

A few days before the fight Barton rounded up the bulls and drove them into the new pens. The five bullfighters arrived with Attorney Moore, their sponsor. The town took on a festive air.

Alonzo B. Webster

The town to-night presents a strange appearance. Cowboys from all over the entire west and southwest are here to see the coming event. Hundreds are present from the east . . . Play runs high and heavy bets are being made. It is indeed a gala season here, and a gala season at Dodge is unlikely to be witnessed elsewhere in the world. There are few towns like Dodge. Here the people rule to suit themselves. Prohibition is the law of the state, but it is not the law of Dodge. Saloons, gambling rooms and dance halls run with perfect freedom, and their proprietors are the leading men of the town. The audacity of the town is wonderful. Where is there another town in the country that would have the nerve to get up a genuine Spanish bull fight on American soil? Dodge has its own laws, and these laws are rigidly inforced . . . People in the east have formed the idea that Dodge is still the embodiment of all the wickedness in the southwest and that it is dangerous for a stranger to come into the town . . . The impression however, is a false one. Dodge is a rough frontier town and it is populated largely by rough people, but they are not at all vicious . . . I would have less fear of molestation in this wild western town than I would have on the side streets of Kansas City or Chicago late in the evening.

New York Herald, July, 1884

Mexican bullfighters at Dodge City, July 4, 1884

On the morning of July 4, 1884, the streets were jammed with people. Businesses going full blast assured the backers of the financial success of the bullfight. At 2 o'clock Webster, Moore and the matadors led the procession to the fairgrounds. Behind them came the town dignitaries followed by the famous Cowboy Band. The bullfighters in red jackets, blue tunics, white stockings and small dainty slippers delighted the crowd with their unique appearance.

At 2:45 the audience commenced filing into the amphitheater, at least one-third of them being women and children. As some of the ladies of the town are not remarkable for sanctity, a dividing line was carefully drawn by a deputy sheriff detailed for that purpose . . . The heat was intense, and parasols and umbrellas were worth their weight in gold . . . Opposite the good citizens were seated the gentlemen of the cattle interest, with their girls, the cowboys ambition seemed to be to get a big fat girl and a high seat at the same time.

Dodge City Democrat, July 5, 1884

The bugle sounded and the first bull entered the arena. He was a red, fierce looking brute full of fight. As he passed through the gate two decorated barbs were thrown into his neck just below each horn. Captain Gallardo, chief matador, began making successful passes at the bull. Other fighters entered to display their skills. As they closed in the bull rushed and another festooned dart hung from his shouldlers. Time and again the bull charged until his back and sides were decorated with a floating sea of colored streamers from his horns to his tail.

Eventually he was driven back to the pens. The second bull proved to be a coward and soon was taken out. The third and fourth were also disappointing and the fifth bull was the worst of all getting stuck in the chute and having to be whipped out by the cowboys. By this time the crowd demanded that the first bull be returned. Again began the sweep of the cape and the wheel and charge of the bull. Suddenly Gallardo was down with the bull's horns inches away, quickly he crawled to safety behind the guard. Gallardo regained his composure; bowed and signaled the band to resume the music for swording. Approaching the bull, Gallardo continued the parley until finally he struck and penetrated the vital spot. The bull staggered a pace or two, stumbled to his knees and then sank to the ground. Thus ended the first day's bullfight in Dodge City, and for all we know the first on American soil.

The bullfight showed outsiders that Dodge was still wild and bucking. But for all their bravado, the citizens knew better. The promoters had unknowingly officiated at the death of one era in Dodge and the birth of another.

Robert M. Wright

He was called "Mr. Dodge City." Everybody in Kansas knew Bob Wright and every important visitor to Dodge City met him. Wright was a cosmopolitan frontiersman who spoke the language of soldiers, buffalo hunters and freighters, but who was equally at home with railroad officials, governors, senators and eastern businessmen.

Robert M. Wright, an adventurer, came West seeking his own destiny. He was born in Maryland in 1840 and at the age of 16 ventured to St. Louis where he spent three years working at various jobs. In 1859 he went farther west into Kansas Territory as a contractor and overseer on the Santa Fe Trail. His new job entailed putting up stations, cutting hay and hauling grain; and took him the length of the trail in Kansas to the Colorado border. After 1865 Wright settled at Fort Dodge and became, along with his job of overseer, the operator of the Sutler Store.

Wright, Beverly Co. 1883

Robert M. Wright

Wright, one of the leading forces in the founding of Dodge City, was chosen president of the Town Company. Over the years he had been a freighter, stage line operator, Indian fighter and wood contractor; but it was as a shipper of buffalo hides and outfitter of hunters, cowhands and cattlemen that Wright became wealthy. Later, he was a cattleman and wheat farmer.

Wright's initiative and foresight as well as his restless vigor played a large part in making Dodge the leading trading, shipping and merchandising center of the Southwest. Wright regularly sent agents down the trail to tell the Texas drovers of the ease with which Dodge could handle their business; and even made personal trips to talk to the cattlemen. In 1880 he had circulars printed which he sent south assuring the cattlemen the trail was open and Dodge was ready for them.[3]

During the town's growing years, two opposing groups were in a continuous struggle as to the kind of town they wanted Dodge to be. Bob Wright, Bat Masterson and the remnants of the Old Dodge City "Gang" wanted the town to remain wide open — a sporting man's town catering to what was left of the cattle trade. The prohibitionists and most of the merchants, led by Mike Sutton and Nick Klaine, felt that the future of Dodge lay in selling gingham and hay rakes, not whiskey and .45 caliber ammunition. In 1885 the anti-gang faction complained to the governor, asking for his help in closing the saloons and in cleaning up the town.

Robert Wright wrote to Governor Martin trying to discredit the prohibitionist element.

> *Governor, you have been imposed upon by a lot of soreheads of this town. This gang only consists of about a dozen who breed all the trouble here and continually keep things in hot water, they are public disturbers and agitators and a curse to any community — who want everyone to think and do as they say — who if they can't rule want to ruin, who do not hesitate to lie and prevaricate to gain their selfish ends, who pretend to be Moralists but are wolves in sheep's clothing, in short they are hypocrites of the deepest and darkest kind. Such even is M. W. Sutton, N. B. Klaine ... and a few others of the kind ... I know them and I know well their dirty black hearts, which never beat with a single generous thought for their fellow man. Sutton is a good lawyer and I admire his ability, but I know his motives. He pretends to be a great temperance man and he drinks more whiskey in a week than I do in a year. Now Governor, these are the men who have caught your ear and I assure you I have not pictured them half as mean and contemptible as they really are.[4]*

The governor sided with Sutton and Klaine rather than Wright; and on November 24, Attorney General Bradford arrived in Dodge to close the saloons. While Bradford was in town the watering holes were closed. He left Dodge on the 26th and the following morning the saloons opened for business as usual.

That same night, November 27, 1885, a fire of mysterious origin started in an upstairs room over the Junction Saloon. It was soon out of control and a whole block on Front Street, including the Junction, the Opera House, the Long Branch and Bob Wright's brick store building burned to the ground. Even as hundreds of men fought to contain the fire, the rumor spread that it had been started by the prohibitionists. At four o'clock in the morning, while flames still licked at his demolished store, Mayor Wright pumped three shots into Mike Sutton's house. Wright later claimed that many threats had been made that awful night against Sutton and others and that he had gone to the house to protect Sutton's family. He fired, he said, at a prowler. An uneasy truce prevailed in the political and social war during that winter; but politics in Dodge flared and simmered around Wright and others for many years.[5]

Robert Wright, influential leader during Dodge City's growing years, was a state legislator from Ford County for several terms; he also was mayor, postmaster and county treasurer. Always concerned about improvng Dodge, Wright deeded a parcel of land to the city for a park which later was named for him.

Robert Wright was married at St. Louis in 1859 and was the father of eight children. After his wife's death Wright married again and they had one son, Connor. During his later years Robert Wright wrote a book of his remembrances of frontier life, *DODGE CITY, THE COWBOY CAPITAL*, a classic reference book of early days in southwest Kansas. Though Wright had been prosperous—even wealthy—most of his life, he died practically penniless, in 1915, of pneumonia.

BEN HODGES

Among the many characters who rode the trail into Dodge City, Benjamin F. Hodges occupied a pedestal all by himself. There was not a single other character in his class.

Ben Hodges, self-proclaimed outlaw and horse and cattle thief, came up the cattle trail to Dodge with the Barton brothers following one of the first herds from Texas. He was shrunken and beady-eyed; his shuffling walk caused, he said, from having his hamstrings cut for stealing horses.

He talked in a loud shrill voice which broke into a cackle at the end of each sentence. Though he never learned to read or write, Ben could print his name. He boasted that the blood of three races — Spanish, Negro and Indian — coursed through his veins. He also boasted that he was one of the heirs to a vast old Spanish land grant.

In the early 1880's some Dodge City cattlemen heard that Mexican heirs had revived their claims to an old Spanish land grant where the Hodges family originated. About this same time Ben returned from a trip to Texas and presented himself carrying papers that showed him not only as a claimant, but also as a representative of the other heirs. Most of the businessmen supported Ben as insurance against calamity in case his claim actually bore fruit. They gave him unlimited credit and he lived high on the hog.

Ben had a grand time in Gray County claiming ownership of thirty-two sections of land with a valuable document which supposedly was destroyed in the Front Street fire. He wrangled a free pass on the railroad and even had a swing at politics. An Emporia judge, impressed by the claims, tried to help settle the case; but when some local men wrote of Ben's true character, the Land Grant Case was thrown out of court.

As the years went by Ben shuffled along the streets, a red handkerchief around his neck, a big dirty white hat pulled down over his ears, carrying a market basket over his arm to collect handouts. The basket concealed a long six-gun from which the firing pin had been removed. Before Thanksgiving one year, Ben told a businessman, "All you folks are going to have ducks and nice things for Thanksgiving dinner, but ol' Ben will just have stew." The man took Ben into a grocery store and told the butcher to give Ben a duck. Ben insisted on a live one, not one of those "packin' house" ducks, so a live one was set aside for him. Ben left the store and the man paid for the duck saying, "Well, that will make a nice Thanksgiving dinner for Ben." The butcher answered, "It should. He has eleven more in the back room."[6]

Ben lived in a shack on the river bank which had been given to him by George M. Hoover. The little building had no windows and only a piece of black oilcloth for a door; but it was jealously guarded against trespassers by Ben, his shotgun and a bulldog named Venus. The shack burned one cold night in the winter of 1929. Ben was taken to the hospital and died several weeks later.

The townspeople who had humored and supported Ben, collected money so that he could be buried in a casket; but there was not enough money to buy a tombstone. His grave remained unmarked until 1965 when a stone was purchased by the Ford County Historical Society with donations from people who had known or heard of Ben Hodges.

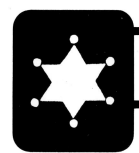 # LAW AND ORDER

Dodge City, from its birth in 1872, was a wild reckless town. Buffalo hunters who swarmed over the plains and soldiers from the nearby fort came to Dodge to buy supplies, to drink and play away their boredom.

County officials, such as a sheriff, could not be elected until Ford County was legally established in 1873. Dodge City could not elect officials until it was incorporated in 1875. Before 1873 Ford County's law enforcement was in Hays City more than 100 miles away. That is the reason citizens of Dodge formed a vigilante committee; however its leadership gradually shifted from reputable to disreputable men whose methods were no better than of those outside the law.

Fortunately the county soon was established and Charles Bassett was elected the first sheriff. Elections for sheriff were held every two years, and the officer was allowed to serve only two consecutive terms. This two-term law explains why two men would turn about as sheriff and undersheriff succeeding each other for a number of terms. (This was changed in 1966 when a new state law allowed a sheriff to succeed himself an unlimited number of times.) The sheriff appointed an undersheriff as his assistant and a number of deputies as they were needed, sometimes for only a day or two.

In 1876 Lawrence Deger, a huge man weighing about 300 pounds, was appointed the first city marshal by George Hoover, the first elected mayor. The terms city marshal and chief of police were interchangeable until 1971 when the city commission designated the chief law enforcement officer as chief of police. At the same time the commission passed a resolution establishing the office of marshal "in order that the historic character and heritage of the city of Dodge City shall be commemorated and continued." Today the office of marshal is honorary and ceremonial and receives no salary.

Through the years the marshal was appointed by the mayor and the city council, except between 1896 and 1901 when he was elected. During the early years the marshal might be appointed for political reasons, but his assistant marshals and deputies were chosen for their abilities to uphold the law and keep the peace. All officers might receive the same salaries, particularly during the peak of the cattle season. Both the marshal and his assistant might be called "marshal."

During the rambunctious years of early Dodge it was a common practice for the county sheriff to appoint city peace officers as undersheriffs or deputies, and in return the city marshal appointed county officers as city policemen.

Because of the high cost of law enforcement, an ordinance was passed calling for fines to be collected from prostitution and gambling establishments. These fines provided ample money to pay for law enforcement.[1]

> The City Council did a wise thing in endeavoring to wipe out the city indebtedness by raising the dram (saloon) shop license from $100 to $300. The city has a debt of nearly $3,000 hanging over it. But while the Council had their eyes on a depleted treasury they also had their attention called to the large pockets of our police force and city attorney, to whom they have allowed an additional amount for their invaluable services. While they left the Chief Marshal's salary at $100, they have raised the salary of the Assistant Marshal and Policeman from $50 to $100 per month, making the expense of the police force $300 per month. When an officer makes an arrest he is allowed a fee of $2.00.
>
> **Ford County Globe, April 15, 1879**

Dodge City is dull at the present time, and the town is relapsing into morality. At this writing there are only seventeen saloons and dance houses, sixty prostitutes, thirty gamblers and eighty cowboys in the entire town.

Dodge City Times, September 15, 1877
(Quoting from the Hays City Sentinel)

Wholesale and Retail

LIQUOR HOUSE.

CONSISTING OF THE

Leading Brands Champagnes,

Brandies,

Whiskies,

Gins,

Rums,

Rhein Wines,

California Wines,

BITTERS.

Milwaukee, Cincinnati and Quincy Beer,

Genuine Apple Cider.

HENRY STURM.

N. B. Livery, Feed and Sale Stable north of the Liquor establishment. Hay, Corn, Oats, and all kinds of feed for sale.

LONG BRANCH SALOON.

DRAKE & WARREN, Proprietors.

WINES,
LIQUORS,
& CIGARS.

Also Billiard Parlor &
a Club Room.

GENERAL HEADQUARTERS OF STOCKMEN.

'THE OASIS.'

(South Side Railroad Track.)

Wm. Tilghman, Proprietor.

OPEN AT ALL HOURS OF DAY OR NIGHT.

THT BEST BRANDS OF LIQUORS AND CIGARS ARE KEPT AT THIS HOUSE.

BRICK BOND.   TOM NIXON.

BOND & NIXON,

Are still supplying their patrons with the best brands of

LIQUORS AND CIGARS,

First class RESTAURANT attached, where Oysters, Game and all delicacies in season will be served.

Old Stand, Corner Second Avenue,

SOUTH SIDE RAILROAD,   DODGE CITY, KANSAS.

G. M. HOOVER,

WHOLESALE DEALER IN

WINES,

Liquors and Cigars,

Genuine Kentucky Bourbon,

SOUR MASH AND KENTUCKY RYE WHISKIES.

MILWAUKEE, QUINCY, AND ST. LOUIS BEER.

ALSO A VARIETY OF CASE GOODS,

Standard and Aromatic Bitters; Case Gin; Fine Imported Cogniac Brandy; Catawba Wine; Cook's Imperial, and other brands of Champagne in quantities to suit any and all customers.

CALL AND EXAMINE.

No. 36, FRONT ST., DODGE CITY, KAS.

"OLD HOUSE" SALOON

AND

LUNCH COUNTER.

Lunch Served at all Hours.

Pure Wines, Liquors and Cigars.

My lean, lank, hungry-looking friend, why don't you take your meal at the 'Old House' Restaur'nt and grow fat?

My friend, I thank you for your kind advice. It is worth a good bit to know where to get a square meal! I will patronize the "Old House."

Opposite Opera House.   -   -   DODGE CITY, KAS.

James "Dog" Kelley, who was elected mayor in 1877, was supported by a remnant of the old frontier element with backgrounds similar to his — buffalo hunters, teamsters, ex-cavalrymen and other border characters. Kelley ran the town in a way that accomodated these people. Saloons, gambling establishments and houses of prostitution ran wide open; but, fines were collected regularly.

1878 was a year never to be forgotten. All of the elements were in Dodge that would provide stories for books, movies and television shows for years to come — spirited cowboys shooting up the town, maurading Indians, a train robbery, the murder of the marshal and of a beautiful belle of the town.

1878

Bat Masterson

Wyatt Earp

Bat Masterson was sheriff of Ford County and Ed Masterson was marshal of Dodge City.

January 27	Train robbery at Kinsley Bat's posse captured two of the robbers
February 10	Posse rode to western Texas looking for more of the robbers. They were gone twelve days but found no suspects.
March 16	Two more of the train robbers arrested in Dodge
April 9	Ed Masterson killed while trying to disarm a cowboy Street fights too numerous to mention Charles Bassett appointed marshal
May & June	Busy capturing horse thieves and returning stolen horses Doc Holliday, dentist, registered at the Dodge House and seeing patients in room No. 24. Money refunded if not satisfied
July 16	Assistant U. S. Deputy Marshal Harry McCarty shot and killed while standing at the bar in the Long Branch
July 26	Cowboy George Hoy tried to shoot up the Lady Gay Saloon, was fatally wounded by Assistant Marshal Wyatt Earp and Policeman Jim Masterson
August 17	Shooting affair at Comique, no one injured
September	Indian scare. The flight of Dull Knife and his small band of Cheyennes, from Oklahoma across western Kansas toward their former home in the Dakotas, threw the citizens of Dodge City into a panic Al Manning shot John Brown in the foot Skunk Curley shot a visitor from Great Bend inflicting an ugly wound Frank Trask, former policeman, shot while crossing the tracks
October 1	Colonel William H. Lewis, commandant at Ft. Dodge, killed while pursuing the Cheyennes in northwest Kansas
October 4	Dora Hand, dance hall singer, killed

Sad News

Dodge City in Mourning

Ed Masterson April 9, 1878

At ten o'clock last night, City Marshal Edward Masterson, discovered that a cowboy named Jack Wagner was carrying a six-shooter contrary to the City Ordinance. Wagner was at the time under the influence of liquor, but quietly gave up the pistol. The Marshal gave it to some of Wagner's friends for safe keeping and stepped out into the street. No sooner had he done so than Wagner ran out after him pulling another pistol, which the Marshal had not observed. The Marshal saw him coming and turned upon Wagner and grabbed hold of him.

Wagner shot Marshal Masterson at once through the abdomen, being so close to him that the discharge set the Marshal's clothes on fire.

Marshal Masterson then shot Wagner.

About this time a man named Walker got mixed up in the fight. It appears he was a boss herder and Wagner was working under him. He also got shot once through the left lung, and his right arm was twice broken.

Wagner, being shot ran into Peacock's saloon and fell upon the floor, where he remained until carried away by friends. He was fatally shot through the abdomen. He died on the evening of the 10th, and was buried on the hill near town (Boot Hill) at 4 P.M. on the eleventh.

Walker, the boss herder, ran through Peacock's saloon and fell some distance in the rear of the saloon from whence he was carried by his friends to a room over Wright Beverly & Co.'s store, where he now lies in a very precarious condition.

Marshal Masterson walked across the tracks and street and entering Hoover's saloon in the agonies of death he said to George Hinkle, "George, I am shot," and sank to the floor. His clothes were still on fire from the discharge of the pistol. He was carried to his brother's room where in half an hour he died.

Everyone in the City knew Ed Masterson and liked him. They liked him as a boy, they liked him as a man, and they liked him as an officer.

The funeral procession marched to the military cemetery at Fort Dodge where last rites were performed.

Dodge City Times and Ford County Globe

Midnight Assassin.

Dora Hand alias Fannie Keenan,
Foully Murdered While in Bed
and Fast Asleep.

On Friday morning October 4, about 4 o'clock, two shots were fired into a small frame building south of the railroad track and back of the Western House, occupied by Miss Fannie Garretson and Miss Fannie Keenan (Dora Hand). The first passed through the front room and lodged in the next room. The second shot also passed through the door, but being apparently more elevated struck the first bed, passing over Miss Garretson, through the partition into the next room, striking Miss Hand in the right side, under the arm, killing her instantly.

The deceased came to Dodge City this summer and was engaged as a vocalist in the Varieties and Comique shows. She was a prepossessing woman and her artful winning ways brought many admirers within her smiles and blandishments. If we mistake not, Dora Hand has an eventful history. She had applied for a divorce from Theodore Hand. After a varied life the unexpected death messenger cuts her down in the full bloom of gayety and womanhood. She was the innocent victim.

The party who committed this cowardly act must have been on horseback and close to the door when the two shots were fired. From what we can learn the shots were intended for another party who has been absent for a week and who formerly occupied the first room (Mayor Kelley). Thus the assassin misses his intended victim and kills another while fast asleep who never spoke a word after she was shot.

James Kennedy, who it is supposed did the shooting made good his escape, and the following morning the officers went in pursuit of him, returning Saturday night with their prisoner, whom they met and on refusal to surrender shot him through the shoulder and with another shot killing the horse he was riding, thus capturing him.

Dodge City Times and Ford County Globe

James Kennedy, the son of Captain Mifflin Kennedy who, along with Richard King owned the fabulously wealthy King Ranch of Texas was acquitted of the murder of Dora Hand for lack of evidence. The posse that captured Kennedy was made up of some of the West's legendary lawmen — Bat Masterson, Wyatt Earp, Bill Tilghman and Charles Bassett.

The story of Dora Hand has been told and retold in books about Dodge City and the West, but no more is known about her today than was known in October 1878. Dora Hand still is a woman of mystery.

Dodge City War

In the spring of 1881 free and easy Mayor Kelley was defeated by Alonzo B. Webster, a moderate reformer who was supported by some of the businessmen and moral reformers. These two factions the old frontier "anything goes" vs. the new "let's make this a decent town," influenced politics for many years to come.

Webster's reforms began immediately and lasted two years, since he was reelected in 1882. Prostitution was not abolished, but was stripped of its flagrant trappings — whores were banned from saloons; no new dance halls were permitted to open. The saloons were not closed even though a prohibition law had been passed in Kansas in 1880.

Lawrence Deger, newly elected mayor in 1883, and the city council passed an ordinance banning prostitution in all public places. Two days later the city police raided the Long Branch Saloon, now owned by W. H. Harris and Luke Short. Three prostitutes (posing as singers) were arrested, jailed and fined while women were allowed to solicit freely in other saloons. This outrageous discrimination against Harris and Short exploded into what became known as the "Dodge City War."

Although the women were arrested peaceably without resistance, Short, later that night exchanged shots in the street with the arresting policeman, L. C. Hartman. Luke Short then was arrested and given his choice of departing trains — east or west. He chose east and traveled to Kansas City and later Topeka where he met with Governor Glick and told his side of the story. Short's account of the facts was picked up by reporters and printed in newspapers across the country. Wyatt Earp, Bat Masterson, Charlie Bassett and other old friends rallied to Short's side and descended on Dodge calling themselves the "Dodge City Peace Commission." Anxious citizens frantically wired the governor asking for State Militia protection. A satisfactory solution ultimately was worked out and Short peacefully resumed business activities in Dodge. However, the national newspaper coverage of the "war" put Dodge in a bad public light. The officials of the Santa Fe Railroad, who had promoted the town as its major shipping point, were displeased with the bad publicity. They issued an ultimatum that if certain moral reforms were not made, the company would revoke the status of Dodge City as a division terminal and cancel plans for future construction.

This new moralistic tone was beginning to be reflected in newspapers.

> Closed. The glaring, glittering and hifalutin' in Dodge is closed, wound-up, suspended. The music hall and the dance hall are of the forgotten past. The last relic of the frontier has given up the ghost. The city council on Friday last passed ordinances requiring the closing of all business on Sunday and abolishing music and singing in saloons and dance halls. The proprietors did not wait until the ordinances became legal by publication, but promptly closed saloons and business houses on Sunday last, having previously discharged musicians and singers . . . Ordinances on gambling and prostitution already exist, and an official order only is required to put these laws in operation. Gambling is now conducted in back rooms, and we presume this vice will be reached by monthly raids, and consequently monthly fines . . .
>
> **Dodge City Times, September 6, 1883**

Although this sounds as if Dodge was closed down tight, nothing could be more wrong. The old Dodge that said, "Hell, we're not in the United States" would not give up her saloons the first time around.

> Thursday evening last the 'joints' were all closed again by order of the City Marshal Rhodes. We suppose someone has made a big 'kick' — our city officials will have to go dry now, as well as the common people of this community, for they will not be able to rush to the 'growler,' as we are informed has been the custom on several occasions. We are creditably informed that at the last meeting of the City Council, the city clerk was ordered by his Honor, the mayor and members of the council to 'rush to the growler', which order was promptly complied with and our city dads regaled themselves with copious draughts of cool and sparkling beer.
>
> **Dodge City Democrat, June 27, 1896**

Prohibition had been a law in Kansas for more than 20 years when saloons again were closed in Dodge City in July 1902 by order of the "Preachers of Dodge City;" and yet again in November 1903 by order of the county attorney.

In 1885, the Kansas legislature began enforcing the Texas cattle quarantine law which made it illegal to drive and ship Texas cattle from points within the state; this along with a stronger prohibition law strengthened the moralists position in Dodge. This was expressed by Judge J. Strang in a letter to the governor,

> ... The quarantine law passed last winter is quietly working out the salvation of Dodge City. The festive cowboy is already becoming conspicuous by his absence in Dodge, and ere long he will be seen and heard there, in his glory, no more forever. The cowboy gone, the gamblers and prostitutes will find their occupations gone, and from necessity must follow. The bulk of the saloons will then die out because there be not sufficient support left, and the temperance people can close the rest as easily as they could in any other city in Kansas.[2]

As Dodge began to settle down, its need for law enforcement decreased and so did the salaries of the peace officers.

> On account of the depleted condition of the city's finances, an ordinance was introduced which cuts the city marshal's salary down to $1 per month. It was stated that the town was quiet and peaceable and that the duties of the marshal were very light. That if the merchants wanted a night watchman they could contribute as they did before to watch their stores at night.
>
> **Dodge City Democrat,** July 21, 1889

Over the years there have been may changes in law enforcement, but Dodge City's unique beginning and struggles are Dodge City's alone.

Boot Hill

For six years, from 1872 to 1878, Dodge had no official cemetery. Persons dying there, who had friends, relatives and especially money, were buried in the cemetery at Fort Dodge. Others of no consequence were stripped of valuables, rolled in blankets and buried, not always on Boot Hill, but any place around town. This explains why bodies or bones are sometimes found when excavations are made or during street work. In 1904 a Chinese man came to Dodge offering a reward for the remains of his brother who was buried in a downtown street.

Boot Hill stood boldly over the new little town and was a convenient spot for burials. In its original state, before the south side was cut away and any buildings had been erected, Boot Hill was a prominent bluff made of gypsum, rock, clay and sand, covered with buffalo grass and decorated with clumps of soapweed and prickly pear.

George M. Hoover recalled that the first burial on Boot Hill was in September, 1872. A black man, known only as Black Jack, was shot in the head and killed instantly by a gambler named Denver in front of Beatty and Kelley's saloon and restaurant. "He was planted, as they called it, with his boots on on Boot Hill and it at all times carried that name. During the winter of 1872 and spring of '73 no less than fifteen men were killed in Dodge City and were planted on Boot Hill."[3]

As far as is known only one woman was buried there — Alice Chambers a dance hall girl. We know something about Alice because she was mentioned often in the newspapers and court records. In October, 1876 Dr. Galland treated her for an unknown ailment, and in January the doctor filed suit against her to collect $15.75 for the medical services. Dr. Galland's suit was settled after a year and he was allowed $2.00 on the medical bill. In the meantime, in March the *Dodge City Times* reported, "On Wednesday a gust of wind removed seven dollars out of the stocking of Alice Chambers as she was walking up Front Street." In July, 1877 Assistant Marshal Ed Masterson arrested Alice for fighting with Miss Howe, alias Dutch Kate, Alice was fined $3.00 plus $12.90 court costs. Masterson earned $2.00 for making the arrest. In August Alice was sued again for a medical bill, this time by Dr. McCarty and Dr. Tremaine for $30.20. To prevent the court from taking her house on Walnut Street (now Gunsmoke) to pay the bill, Alice deeded it to her "live in friend," gambler Charles Ronan. Eight months later, May 1878, Alice was dead.

There have been stories about the huge funeral given by the town for one of its favorites. But Emelie Mueller Chambliss, daughter of John Mueller the bootmaker, who saw the procession as a little girl, said there were only a few men behind J. C. Overly's dray wagon. Alice was the last person to be buried on Boot Hill and the only woman.

Few of the old-timers have told of witnessing burials there. The victims usually were killed during the night's revelry and thrown into an alley or street. The city marshal, with his helpers, usually dug the grave, and the burial took place the following morning.

Early in 1879 the bodies were removed from Boot Hill to make way for a new school building, and were reburied in Prairie Grove, the first official cemetery in Dodge.

> The skeltons removed from the graves on Boot Hill were found to be in a fine state of preservation, and even the rude box coffins were sound as when placed in the ground. Colonel Straughn, the coroner, who removed them, says they were as fine a collection of the extinct human race as he ever handled. Some were resting with their boots on, while others made more pretentions to style, having had their boots removed and placed under their heads for pillows. Only a few of them could be recognized, as all of their headboards, if there ever were any, had long since wasted away and nothing remained to denote where their bodies lay but little mounds of clay. They are now all resting side by side like one happy family, at the lower end of Prairie Grove cemetery northeast of the city. The enchanting click of the festive revolver they no longer hear. The sighs of the Kansas zephyrs are unheeded and the sportive grasshopper, perched on a headboard, chews his cud and chants his harvest song without the fear of God in his heart.
>
> **Ford County Globe, February 4, 1879**

The new Third Ward or Boot Hill School was dedicated February 4, 1880. Attorney Mike Sutton made the principal address. In his speech he remembered,

> *In 1872 a man was shot in a row within a few yards of where the speaker now stands. The body lay nearly all day without anyone to care for it, when towards evening a grave was dug upon the identical spot where we have built the new school building. The grave thus made, was followed by many others, until the beautiful hill became dotted with little mounds to the number of twenty-five or thirty, and the hill itself was named Boot Hill because nearly all of the tenants of its graves were buried in their boots.*
>
> **Ford County Globe, February 10, 1880**

In 1890 the Third Ward building was found to be poorly constructed. It was demolished and the material used to erect a second building on the same site. This school was razed in 1928 and a Spanish style City Hall was built. The cowboy statue which stands in front of this building was made by Dr. O. H. Simpson, a pioneer dentist, to commemorate the frontier days of the cattle drives. The marker on the statue states:

"On the ashes of my campfire this city is built."

Chalk Beeson

Chalk Beeson left his home in Ohio to go to Colorado when he was 19 years old. In 1872 while Bob Wright and others were busy getting Dodge City organized, Beeson was a member of the Royal Buffalo Hunt which was arranged to entertain the Grand Duke Alexis of Russia. Beeson was invited to go on the hunt after he was overheard by General Phil Sheridan and General Custer boasting that he knew where the best hunting was to be found.

Two years later Beeson came to Dodge City and became the proprietor of the Long Branch Saloon and a town leader. He was representative from Ford County for six years, and was elected sheriff for two terms.

Besides being an experienced frontiersman and professional musician, Beeson was an astute businessman and a genial saloon host. Men of distinction made the Long Branch their headquarters. The saloon, where no dancing was allowed, maintained a high-toned sporting atmosphere. Mr. Beeson, who was determined to make his establishment a center of culture as well as a place for thirsty cowpunchers, provided first class music for the customers with a four piece orchestra.[4]

Chalk Beeson organized the 18 member Dodge City Cowboy Band in 1878. It was financed by members of the local cattlemen's association, and each musician displayed on his Stetson hat the cattle brand of an individual sponsor. The musicians wore blue-flannel shirts and bandana handkerchiefs. Their leather chaps were held up by cartridge belts. Sixteen inch six-shooters and spurs on the boots completed their colorful outfits.

The band made national news when it appeared at the Stockmen's Convention at St. Louis in 1884. After watching the leader direct with a pistol, a fascinated reporter from the *St. Louis Globe-Democrat* asked:

"What do you swing that gun for?"
"That's my baton," was the answer.
"Is it loaded?"
"Yes."
"What for?" the reporter asked.
"To kill the first man who strikes a false note," the leader solemnly assured the newspaperman.[5]

Following its triumph at the Cattlemen's convention, the band received an invitation to visit Chicago. While there the band, dressed in full regalia, played daily concerts in the exclusive Palmer House.

In 1889 Beeson took the Cowboy Band to Washington, D.C. for the inauguration of President Benjamin Harrison. By this time the members had put aside their leather chaps for woolly ones, attracting more attention than ever. The easterners were fascinated and impressed with the band's performance and antics. When questioned if the band members were really cowboys, Chalk Beeson said, "I have boys in our band who can throw a steer over a horse." However, others said the musicians were professionals from theaters and dance halls in Denver, Kansas City, St. Louis and Chicago. Whatever the true story, The Dodge City Cowboy Band was one of the unique institutions of western Kansas and was a successful promoter for Dodge City. After the inaugural trip the band broke up. The band charter and paraphernalia were sold to Jack Sinclair, Idaho Springs, Colorado.

Chalk Beeson, who was an expert horseman, was thrown by a young unruly animal. He died a week later on August 9, 1912. His sons built the Beeson Theater as a memorial to their father. The building, no longer used as a theater, is on the corner of First and Gunsmoke Streets. Many items from the Long Branch Saloon and from the Beeson family may be seen in the Boot Hill Museum.

THE DODGE CITY COWBOY BAND
Chalk Beeson is seated second from
the right in the front row

FRONT STREET VIEW OF CENTRAL BLOCK, DODGE CITY, 1887

GROWING UP

Dodge City was forced to grow up. By the middle 1880's the cattle drives from Texas had ended; Fort Dodge was closed as a military post; open lands were turned into farms by homesteaders. Businesses were converting from cattle to a farm centered economy. The town was on its way to growth and prosperity when the disasters of 1885 and 1886 changed the face of Front Street as well as the economy of the old Dodge.

There had been minor fires in Dodge, some under the board sidewalks. Because many of the saloons and businesses never closed, someone was always around to discover the fires in time for them to be put out by the bucket brigade. Then on January 18, 1885 a fire started which was too much for frontier fire fighting. Eight business houses north of the tracks and several warehouses south of the tracks were destroyed.

Ten months later during the night of November 27, 1885 a fire started in a room over the Junction Saloon that wiped out the heart of the business district, the block that housed Wright's store and Kelley's Opera House. Besides these two businesses, two drug stores, a mercantile company, three saloons, a furniture store, a jewelry store and a hardware store were burned to the ground.

Ten days later on, December 7, fire destroyed another block of buildings which included a newspaper shop, several stores and residences.

Only three weeks after this fire, the first blizzard struck. New Year's Eve had been celebrated joyously, but revelers awoke New Year's Day to a blinding blizzard with temperatures ten to twenty degrees below zero. The storm lasted almost four days.

Thirteen days later the second blizzard, far worse than the first, came howling out of the north. This storm lasted only half as long, but the snow was heavy. A train with 80 passengers was snowbound a few miles east of Dodge City for five days.

Local businessmen who had invested heavily in cattle were devastated. The melting snow revealed the reality of their losses; carcasses piled three and four deep; the remaining animals staggered about on frozen feet. Losses in Ford County were estimated at 60 to 80 percent. Many ranchers were ruined. John Mueller was forced to return to bootmaking, 7,000 acres of land belonging to Bob Wright were sold for taxes. Ford County now turned more to crop farming as opposed to the gamble of cattle.

After the cruel winter of 1886 the city fathers got back to the job of improving the services provided by Dodge City.

Services

Fire Department

From the 1870's Dodge had a fire company, but it was primarily an athletic and social club to which the members paid dues to belong. The Fire Company sponsored balls and patriotic celebrations on Washington's birthday and the Fourth of July. Many of the prominent men of the town belonged. The honor escort at Ed Masterson's funeral was made up of his fellow volunteer firemen. The Fire Company was divided into three teams each of which had fifteen members. Team leaders were R. M. Wright, A. B. Webster and A. J. Arment. The teams trained to be able to pull the hose cart and hook up the hose connections in record time.

Hose carts were two wheeled affairs each carrying a huge reel of hose. Eleven members of a team were attached by shoulder and breast harnesses to a rope arrangement by which the cart was pulled. Four men ran behind the cart to unreel the hose and attach it to the pump or fire hydrant. The fire pump was an apparatus on wheels with pump handles on either side connected to cylinders by which a surprising amount of water could be raised from the shallow wells.

Dodge City Hose Cart Team

Tournaments were held between hose teams from rival towns. These events were gala occasions with teams dressed in colorful uniforms racing to see who could run a specified distance and have a hose ready to play on a fire in the shortest time. In 1887 a Dodge City hose team won the national championship at the annual Firemen's Tournament at Denver. The contest rules required the teams to run 450 feet, stretch 100 feet of hose, connect it to a fire hydrant, attach a nozzle and spray the water 20 feet. The Dodge City team whose time was just short of 32 seconds not only won, but established a world's record.

The same year Dodge made its name in the hose cart race, the volunteer fire department gained official status by city ordinance and downtown buildings were required to be constructed with twelve inch brick walls and roofs of metal or slate. In 1914 the city purchased its first motorized fire truck; in 1921 it began paying the firemen for each fire call; and in 1936 a full time paid fire department was created by ordinance.

Water

Dodge City's first water came from the Arkansas River hauled in a tank truck and delivered for 5¢ a bucket. Before long, wells were put down at the intersections of the streets. They were dug in the center of intersections so that horse teams could be watered easily. The driver of a team would stop, get out, and by means of a rope over a pulley supplied with two buckets, draw up all the water needed. Many residents depended on these wells to supply water for their homes.

1887	Water service became available from a private company. Some homes kept their own water wells.
	The first sewer line was laid from the corner of First and Chestnut Streets to the Arkansas River.
1910	The city began operating its own water service. The first big city water well was dug.
1912-1917	The sewer lines were completed.
	Today the city owns and maintains the water services.

Streets

1886	All streets were dirt. Third Avenue was impossible to cross after a rain because it was the floodgate for runoff from the entire west side of town. Mud would become a foot or more deep.
	The first tax money was levied for the opening and grading of streets.
1912	Curb and guttering began. While the hilly streets made sewer laying easier and less expensive, the hills made the installation of curbs and gutters quite difficult because of severe washouts.
1913	Street paving began. The bricks, produced at Buffalo, Kansas, were laid over a six inch concrete base which was covered with a one inch sand cushion. Third Avenue was paved first because of its bad condition.

Gas

1886	Ordinance passed to permit gas lines. Nothing more done until
1908	A charter was issued to George M. Hoover to provide gas service to citizens of Dodge City
1920's	A franchise was given to a commercial gas company.

Gas service now is provided by People's Natural Gas.

Electricity

1886	A few electric lights were turned on. Electricity was provided by the Dodge City Incandescent Electric Light Company owned by R. M. Wright and Brick Bond.
1887	Some downtown street corners which had previously been illuminated by gas lights were lighted by electricity.

Merchants advertised the advantages of shopping in electrically lighted stores.

1904	The franchise was sold to the Midland Water, Light and Ice Company to extend service to the entire community and install more street lights.
1925	Charter was grated to the Kansas Power Company (now West Plains Energy).

Telephone

1880	Robert Wright and Dr. T. L. McCarty installed telephones between their homes and their places of business.
1904	Telephone service became available in Dodge City from a private company.
1920	Southwestern Bell Telephone purchased the local company.

Railroads

During the late 1800's and early 1900's there was considerable railroad expansion. Of these companies which built or planned to build through Dodge City, only two were lasting, the Santa Fe and the Rock Island:

Atchison, Topeka and Santa Fe	Arkansas, Kansas and Colorado
The Rock Island	Omaha, Dodge City and Southern
Chicago, Nebraska, Kansas and Southwestern	Dodge City and Cimarron Valley
Dodge City, Montezuma and Trinidad	Cattle King Railroad Company

Banks

Banks were not needed in early Dodge because local merchants took care of the banking needs. Several banks were opened but closed after a few years. The State Bank of Dodge City, chartered on December 6, 1898, later consolidated with the Kansas State Bank on January 6, 1933 and changed the name to Fidelity State Bank. The State Bank of Commerce opened its doors January 5, 1901, at the corner of First and Front Streets. It became the National Bank of Commerce on June 1, 1904, then changed its name in January 1921 to the First National Bank of Dodge City.

Today Dodge City is served by the Fidelity State Bank and Trust Company, the First National Bank and Trust Company and the Bank of the Southwest.

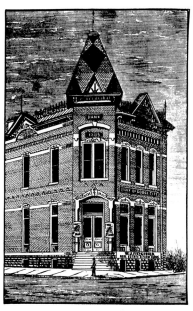

First National Bank

Library

1886	A meeting held at the Union Church to discuss a library resulted in the first public library being set up in the office of the County Superintendent of Instruction. It was open only on Saturdays.
1900	The *Globe Republican* stated that it was "a proper thing to establish a public library in Dodge City."
1905	A group began meeting to campaign for a library
1907	The Dodge City Public Library was built on the corner of Second and Spruce Streets, funded by the city and a grant from the Carnegie Foundation.
	Today the Public Library is located at 1001 Second Avenue

Public Schools

1873	The first school was begun in a little one room frame building on the corner of First and Walnut (Gunsmoke) Streets now the site of the Southwestern Bell Telephone Company.
1880	Third Ward School was built on Boot Hill.
1886	Second Ward School was built on Railroad Avenue (Central)

1887	First high school graduation took place
1890	Third Ward School was rebuilt on the same Boot Hill location
1910	First Ward School was built in east part of town
1915	High School was built on Second Avenue (now USD No. 443 Administration Building). School organized in the Mexican Village.
1921	Coronado School was built in the Mexican Village on the Fort Dodge Road
1920	Sunnyside School was built
1925	Lincoln School was built on West Cedar Street to replace the Boot Hill School
1927	Central School was built to replace the old Second Ward School
1928	The present High School on First Avenue was completed
1951	Miller School was built to replace Roosevelt School in First Ward
1957	Northwest School and a new Junior High School were built

Today Dodge City has seven public elementary schools, one junior high school and one high school.

City Government

Kansas has three classes of cities based on population figures. In general, cities with a population of less than 2,000 are third class; 2,000 to 15,000 are second class; and those over 15,000 are designated cities of the first class. This classification has been in effect for nearly a century.

A city or town is divided into political wards for voting purposes (now called precincts in Dodge City). This explains the names of the first schools in Dodge City—Third Ward School was located in the third political ward and so on.

1875	Dodge City was incorporated and adopted a mayor-council plan of local government.
1886	Dodge City was designated a city of the second class by proclamation of the governor.

The city council was made up of two councilmen elected from each ward. At this time there were three wards so six councilmen plus the mayor were elected.

1887	Women were allowed to vote in city and school elections.
1911	As Dodge City grew, more wards were added until the number of councilmen became unmanageable. The city voted to change from the council system to a three man commission (including the mayor). The commissioners enacted ordinances, appropriated money and adopted revenue measures. One commissioner was in charge of finance and revenue; another was responsible for streets and public utilities. Each was paid $250 a year. The mayor who controlled the police and fire departments received a salary of $300 a year. The mayor presided over the commission meetings, but he did not have veto power. He was merely one of the commissioners in transacting business. The mayor and commissioners were not elected by wards, but by the city at large.
1912	An amendment to the Kansas constitution gave women full voting privileges. The United States Constitution was not amended until 1920.
1970	The citizens of Dodge City voted to change to a city manager-commission plan of government. Under this plan the commissioners do not have charge of departments, but employ a city manager who performs the administrative work. The commission acts as a legislative and policy making body for the city.
1972	The city expanded from a three member to a five member commission. The mayor, no longer elected by the voters, is a commissioner and is chosen by the other members to serve as mayor for one year.
1977	Dodge City became a city of the first class.

His Honor The Mayor

Dodge City's first mayor was P. L. Beatty, a saloon keeper. He was not elected, but appointed at a citizen's mass meeting and took office November 2, 1875, the same day the town, with a few hundred citizens, was incorporated.

George M. Hoover, an outstanding businessman, was the first elected mayor. James H. Kelley, the mayor who followed Hoover, was only one of the colorful characters to preside over "the delectable burg." Kelley came to Fort Dodge as an employee in charge of General George Custer's horses and greyhound dogs. When the 7th Cavalry moved out, Kelley, who had been given the nickname "Dog," stayed to become a leader in Dodge. He owned a saloon, restaurant and opera house. Like many of the frontiersmen Kelley died penniless, a city street laborer. He is buried in the Fort Dodge Cemetery.[1]

Adolph Gluck

Short, round, Adolph Gluck, a wholesale jeweler from St. Louis, was the only mayor to be impeached. He was accused of breaking the prohibition law by having knowledge that liquor was being served in a certain building (his own) and doing nothing to prevent the sales. The mayor was no more guilty than most prominent business men who also knew that liquor was readily available; but he was the victim of a grudge fight by R. N. Hutchinson, an ice dealer. Hutchinson refused to pay the occupation tax required by city ordinance from local businesses. Mayor Gluck harassed him; and Hutchinson fought the tax until he was forced to pay. But, he swore to get Gluck's scalp! It was Hutchinson who brought the prohibition charge against the mayor and asked for his impeachment. At the trial the jury returned the verdict of guilty; however, the voters, unimpressed by the trial, elected Gluck for the next term and then again several years later.[2]

Hamilton B. Bell, mayor of Dodge City from 1912 to 1915, was sheriff of Ford County for twelve years and U. S. Deputy Marshal for almost twelve years, having been appointed to replace Bat Masterson. Western writers looking for a two-gun sheriff and marshal to be the leading man in their books have overlooked Bell; but the truth is, he lived too long for journalists to be able to corrupt his life story into the mythical frontier marshal role.

Ham Bell was born in Maryland and came west when he was nineteen years old. He spent two years in Great Bend as a peace officer and came to Dodge City in 1874. He bought a livery stable, and from this time until after the turn of the century when horses were no longer needed, the stable was his main business. During the cattle seasons the loft of his barn was full of cowboys who were unable to get hotel rooms. Bell's horse-drawn hearse was used for many early Dodge City funerals.

In 1885 Ham Bell built the huge Elephant Barn, 85 feet by 125 feet, on the corner of Fourth and Trail Streets. This largest building in western Kansas was headquarters for cowboys, cattlemen, freighters and wagon caravans. Bell was the owner of the Ham Bell Varieties, a dance hall south of the railroad tracks, where Dora Hand and Eddie Foy performed. Just east of the barn he and Henry Sitler later erected the Sitler-Bell Building where he engaged in the furniture and undertaking business.

Bell was the first automobile dealer in town, selling Chalmers vehicles. He also operated Dodge City's first motorized ambulance and hearse. In 1927 he built the brick structure at 209 West Spruce where he kept an elaborate pet shop. Many local residents, who as children visited Bell's shop, have fond memories of this kindly-eyed soft-spoken old man.

As mayor, Ham Bell began the street paving program and during his administration more than $95,000 in bonds for city improvements were issued, an astounding amount for that time. It has been said the women's vote in 1912 elected handsome, courtly Ham Bell as mayor of Dodge City.

When he was in his 80's, the annual Ham Bell Pioneer Picnic became a county-wide attraction. He traveled to

Hollywood when the movie "Dodge City" was being filmed and was instrumental in securing the premiere for the town. During World War II a B-26 bomber was christened "Ham Bell" and was dedicated in his name. Bell died in 1947 at the age of 94.

GEORGE M. HOOVER, FOUNDER OF DODGE AND
LEADING CITIZEN, DIED LAST EVENING

The funeral of the late G. M. Hoover will be held from the residence at 100 Military Avenue at 2 o'clock tomorrow afternoon. The body will lie in state at the residence from 10 o'clock until 2 tomorrow and friends will view it there. The services will be in charge of Father Floyd Keeler of the Episcopal Church . . .

The banks will close at noon tomorrow and remain closed the remainder of the day out of respect to the memory of the oldest banker in town . . .

Dodge City Daily Globe,
July 16, 1914

This funeral notice reflects the high esteem the city held for George M. Hoover. Few citizens of Dodge City have contributed as much to the community as its first elected mayor.

George Hoover said he had made his money in Dodge City and he was going to leave it here. At the time of his death Hoover's estate was estimated to be a quarter of a million dollars. He left $100,000 in a trust fund to the city of Dodge City with the condition the interest would be used for beautifying the city, park and cemetery. One thousand dollars was left to each of the six churches, as well as money to build the Hoover Pavilion in Wright Park.

On June 17, 1872, Hoover a 25 year old Canadian, with his business partner John McDonald, pitched a tent near Sitler's sod house and opened a saloon. In that day a saloon keeper was considered an aristocrat of the town. Saloon keeping was not only a legitimate occupation, it was looked upon as a respectable profession. Hoover also was a wholesale liquor dealer which was a very profitable business supplying the saloons in early Dodge.

When Hoover moved his wholesale liquor store and saloon north of the tracks he located it one door east of the Long Branch. He ran a simple bar, mainly to accomodate his wholesale customers. He did not allow dancing or gambling except for an occasional game of cribbage. Hoover's wholesale trade extended into Indian Territory and Texas. In August, 1882, one shipment to Tascosa, Texas consisted of 30 barrels of beer, 10 barrels of whiskey, 10,000 cigars and a large lot of keg and case goods which was shipped by H. B. Bell's fast freight.[3]

Hoover opened the Bank of Dodge City in 1882 and was its president for many years. It was the forerunner of Fidelity State Bank. Besides serving four terms as mayor, Hoover was elected twice to the state legislature from Ford County and was a county commissioner several times.

Mr. Hoover's wife, Margaret, was a florist and the story is told that Hoover would select some of her best blossoms each morning, presumably as a bouquet for his desk at the bank; but then would leave them for a certain young lady at one of the stores.

Ham Bell happened to learn of this custom and watched the delivery of the flowers one morning. He bought a matching bouquet and took it to the bank to show Mr. Hoover.

"See my bouquet," he said. Hoover looked at it sharply and thought he recognized it as the one he had carefully selected that morning. "Where did you get that?" he asked. "Oh, the clerk over at the store gave it to me. She gives me one every morning."

Hoover was considerably burned up and let his flower girl know he was upset at her for giving away his flowers. Mr. Bell took his time about telling Hoover it was just a joke.[4]

From Hoover's death in 1914 until April 1938 the city council every year placed flowers on his grave in Maple Grove Cemetery in remembrance of his generosity to the city he loved.

Gospel Hill

Dodge is the Deadwood of Kansas. Her incorporate limits are the rendezvous of all the unemployed scallywaggism in seven states. Her principal business is polygamy, her code of morals is the honor of thieves, and decency she knows not . . . Seventeen saloons furnish inspiration and many people become inspired, not to say drunk. She is a merry town and the only visible means of support of a great many of her citizens is rowdyism.

Hays City Sentinel, 1873

The *Kinsley Graphic* called Dodge "Beautiful bibulous Babylon of the frontier." A roving correspondent for the *Washington Evening Star,* in 1878, thought Dodge deserved the fate of Sodom and Gomorrah, and wrote, "Its character is so clearly bad that one might conclude that it is marked for special providential punishment."

It is no wonder that S. A. Newell, a trainman for the Santa Fe, was concerned about the children. In November of 1872 he gathered six of them together into the dining room of the Dodge House and began to teach and sing to them. This was the beginning of Sunday School and church life in Dodge City. While one of the difficulties he faced was that the singing disturbed the hotel guests, the greatest obstacle was indifference. However, with the help of a young woman, Calvina Anthony, a Presbyterian, he held the little group together and by 1874 the class had grown to twenty-five members. *The Central Christian Advocate* claimed to have obtained, in 1874, the names of all the religious people in Dodge — 13 in all!

On June 14, 1874, these thirteen people, representing several denominations, organized a church. They erected a frame building on the corner of First and Spruce Streets to house the congregation. The little one room Union Church could seat about 100 people. It had wooden benches for pews; was heated by a large cast iron stove and lighted by bracket coal oil lamps. The bell from the Union Church is now displayed as part of a memorial fountain on Boot Hill.[5]

The Wicked city of Dodge can at last boast of a Christian organization, a Presbyterian church. It was organized last Sunday a week. We would have mentioned the matter last week but we thought it best to break the news gently to the outside world.

Dodge City Times, June 8, 1878

The Rev. Ormond Wright, a young Presbyterian minister, served the Union Church as well as his own. He was an Easterner and never changed his style to fit frontier standards. Everyday, dressed in a long-tailed frock coat and high silk hat, he visited the business places, saloons and dance halls. He succeeded in gaining the friendship and support of all classes of people.

In 1880 the Presbyterians built a small Gothic-windowed frame church with a bell cupola on Gospel Hill on the corner at Central and Vine Streets.

Presbyterian Church

Two months later, in August 1878, a Methodist group was organized. They continued to use the Union Church building until 1884 when their frame building on the corner of First and Vine Streets was finished. This served until 1913 when it was replaced with a large red brick church at the same location. The parsonage—educational building was added in 1929.

Methodist Church

The third denomination to organize was the Baptists under the leadership of the Rev. N. G. Collins. At first meetings were held in the Union Church every Sunday afternoon and one evening a week. A frame structure with a tall belfry was built at Sixth and Cedar Streets just east of the present Lincoln School. All went well with Rev. Collins and his flock until a depression struck Dodge City. In desperation he asked Walter N. Locke, a merchant, how they could raise $300 as a payment on the church. Locke, who also was an auctioneer, suggested that Collins have the ladies of the church prepare a musical program and provide boxes of food which he would auction off. He promised to round up the boys on Front Street and south of the tracks to buy the boxes.

The ladies entertained the people gathered at the church with a fine program, then the boxes were auctioned. A girl hidden behind the organ kept Locke informed of the money yet to be raised. One box was left and twenty-five dollars still was needed. Looking around the room for a victim, Locke spied Bat Masterson and knocked the box down to him for that amount. Years later when Mr. Locke was in New York City, he and Bat lunched together. Masterson made sure they went to the most expensive restaurant. When the check was brought he gave it to Locke and said, "Locke, that evens up the box supper score."[6]

Baptist Church

Catholic Church

Although occasionally pranks were played on itinerant preachers by riotous cowboys, there is no record of a Catholic priest being so molested; possibly because Catholic services were held in the sleepy Sunday morning hours. The first missionary priest to hold services in Dodge City was Father Felix Swembergh. The Catholics, too, used the Union Church until 1882 when a little white church, costing about $3,500, was built on Gospel Hill on the corner of Central and Cedar Streets. The cowboys contributed to this and other churches as generously as they did to the gambling halls. The Catholic Church was located where the present Sacred Heart Cathedral stands.

The Christian Church, organized in 1886, in its early struggles was housed in several downtown buildings. A large new church building on the corner of Second and Vine Streets were almost finished when it was destroyed by fire on Christmas Eve, 1909. Rebuilding began and a year later the congregation moved into the red brick church which was used for forty-five years.

One more church was founded before 1900. An Episcopal Mission was organized on May 2, 1888. At first the group met in homes, in downtown stores and in the YMCA reading room. The church building, which was completed in 1898, was constructed by volunteer labor and with gifts from the community. The children of the Sunday School gave bake sales and bazaars to earn money to purchase the large stained glass window over the altar. The stone used for the building was from the old Sturm Ice House. St. Cornelius Church, on the corner of First and Spruce Streets, is the oldest church building in Dodge City.

Episcopal Church

Eyeball Witnesses

Even before Dodge City was made famous by television shows, the town was known all over the world because of newspaper stories from the 1870's and 1880's. A Kansas City correspondent in 1877 visited Dodge and reported:

> At 8:30 a.m. we got off at Dodge, slumbering yet in the tranquil stillness of a May morning. In this respect Dodge is peculiar. She wakens from her slumbers about 11 a.m., takes her sugar and lemon at 12 a.m., a square meal at one, commences biz at 2 o'clock, gets lively at 4 and at 10 it is hip-hip-hurrah 'till 5 o'clock in the morning.[7]

Twenty-two newspapers have been published in Dodge City, two of which are still in publication, *The Dodge City Daily Globe* and *The High Plains Journal.* The *Ford County Globe* was founded in 1878 by D. M. Frost and W.N. Morphy. In 1884 the name was changed to the *Globe Live Stock Journal* to serve the cattle industry. The paper merged with the *Ford County Republican* in 1889 to become the *Globe Republican.* In 1910 when J.C. Denious bought an interest in the paper it became the *Dodge City Globe.* Today it is *The Dodge City Daily Globe.*

The *Dodge City Democrat* was founded by W.R. Petillion in 1883. It was named the *Journal Democrat* from 1905 until 1909 when it became the *Dodge City Kansas Journal.* In 1949 it was changed to *The High Plains Journal*, an agribusiness weekly for the Southwest.

Journalism in those early days was flamboyant and political as you can tell from the names of two of the papers, Republican and Democrat. The editors printed stories of personal grudges, attacked their enemies and carried on feuds with the editor of the opposing paper.

In 1884, although Bat Masterson was not a candidate for office, he worked hard to have his favorites elected. One of his tactics was letters to the editors which were printed free of charge. In this election though, he had more to say about the opposition than could be crammed into a letter. Bat's solution was to print and distribute his own newspaper, *Vox Populi*.

The paper which hit the streets a few days before the election, was an abusive but well-written attack on Bat's political enemies. He described Nick Klaine, editor of the Times, as a thief, liar, murderer, rapist, barn burner and poisoner of horses.

The candidates attacked by *Vox Populi* were defeated, while those friendly to Masterson and the "gang" were elected. Having done its job the paper was discontinued after this one issue. Bat wrote, "The *Vox Populi* is no more . . . It said nothing that it is sorry for, and with declaration it says good day."[8]

These Dodge City newspapers, with their colorful stories, are available for you to read on microfilm and in *Great Gunfighters of the Kansas Cowtowns*, a book by Nyle H. Miller and Joseph W. Snell.

Dodge was a Kansas trail town, wild and reckless; the violence that marked its early history is still remembered. Reputations of people who resorted to violence were boosted out of proportion by journalists and authors who enjoyed good stories, even to the extent of spinning the yarns themselves. And it continues today on television. Without these exaggerations the antics of Dodge City and the West might not so easily have achieved its Wild image.

Photograph Credits

Page 1 — Sutler store, Fort Dodge, courtesy Kansas State Historical Society.

Page 3 — Chas. Rath & Co. hide yard, courtesy Boot Hill, Inc.

Page 8 — Buffalo hides, courtesy Kansas State Historical Society.
Charles Rath, Rath Collection, Kansas Heritage Center

Page 11 — Cattle trail map, courtesy Kansas State Historical Society.

Page 12 — Texas Longhorns in Dodge City, Kansas State Historical Society.

Page 13 — Lone Star Saloon ad, courtesy Kansas State Historical Society.

Page 15 — Alonzo B. Webster, courtesy Kansas State Historical Society.

Page 16 — Mexican bullfighters at Dodge City, Kansas State Historical Society.

Page 17 — Dodge City Front Street, courtesy Boot Hill, Inc.

Page 17 — Robert M. Wright, courtesy Boot Hill, Inc.

Page 19-20 — Ben Hodges, Schmidt Collection, Kansas Heritage Center.

Page 22 — Saloon ads, courtesy Kansas State Historical Society.

Page 23 — Bat Masterson, courtesy Boot Hill, Inc.

Page 23 — Wyatt Earp, courtesy Kansas State Historical Society.

Page 25 — Dora Hand, courtesy Kansas State Historical Society.

Page 30 — Dodge City Cowboy Band, courtesy Boot Hill, Inc.

Pages 31-42 — Lithographs on these pages were published in 1887 in a handbook for
the Ford County Immigration Society, and reprinted by The Etrick
Printery. They were also published in the Globe Livestock Journal,
January 31, 1888.

Page 32 — Hose Cart Team, courtesy Boot Hill, Inc.

Page 38 — Adolph Gluck, courtesy Boot Hill, Inc.

Page 42 — Episcopal Church, courtesy St. Cornelius Episcopal Church.

Page 43 — Newspaper banners, courtesy Kansas State Historical Society.

NOTES

Buffalo City

1. David A. Dary, *The Buffalo Book*, 97.
2. "Reminisences by George Hoover," *Dodge City Democrat*, June 19, 1903.
3. Myra E. Hull, "Cowboy Ballads," *Kansas State Historical Quarterly*, Volume VIII, Number 1, 1939
4. Robert M. Wright, *Dodge City, the Cowboy Capital*, 138.
5. Dary, op, cit., 129.
6. Fred Grove, "Rath City, The Speckled Cattle . . .," *The West*, June 1973.
7. Ibid.
8. David K. Strate, *Sentinel to the Cimarron*, 85.
9. The information about Charles Rath was taken from *The Rath Trail* written by Rath's daughter-in-law, Ida Ellen Rath.

Cattle Town

1. Wright, op. cit., 154-56.
2. Ford County Globe, March 12, 1878.
3. Robert R. Dykstra, *The Cattle Towns*, 155.
4. Ibid, 281-82.
5. Odie B. Faulk, *Dodge City, the Most Western Town of All*, 187.
6. High Plains Journal, September 2, 1954.

Information about the bullfight was taken from "The Bull Fight at Dodge," by Kirke Mechem, *Kansas State Historical Quarterly*, Volume II, Number 3, 1933.

Law and Order

1. *Dodge City Times*, August 10, 1878.
2. Dykstra, op. cit., 280.
3. *Ford County Globe*, February 25, 1904.
4. *Dodge City Democrat*, June 19, 1903.
5. *Ford County Globe*, June 25, 1878.
6. Clifford P. Westheimer, "The Dodge City Cowboy Band," *Kansas State Historical Quarterly*, Volume XIX, Number 1, 1951.

Growing Up

1. *Dodge City Journal*, June 30, 1938.
2. *Globe Republican*, September 17, 1891.
3. *Ford County Globe*, August 29, 1882.
4. *Dodge City Journal*, June 16, 1938.
5. *High Plains Journal*, May 6, 1948.
6. *High Plains Journal*, April 2, 1949.
7. Wright, op. cit., 258.
8. *Globe Livestock Journal*, November 11, 1884.

FOR FURTHER READING

Breihan, Carl. *Great Gunfighters of the West.* San Antonio, Naylor, 1962.

Brown, Dee A. *Trail Driving Days.* New York, Scribner, 1952.

Chrisman, Harry E. *Lost Trails of the Cimarron.* Denver, Sage Books, 1961.

Cox, William. *Luke Short and His Era.* Garden City, N.Y., Doubleday, 1961.

Crumbine, Samuel. *Frontier Doctor.* Philadelphia, Dorrance, 1948.

Dary, David. *The Buffalo Book.* Chicago, Sage Books, 1974.

_____. *Cowboy Culture.* New York, Knopf, 1981.

DeArment, Robert. *Bat Masterson.* Norman, University of Oklahoma Press, 1979.

Dixon, Billy. *Life of "Billy" Dixon, Plainsman, Scout and Pioneer.* Dallas, P.L. Turner Company, 1927.

Drago, Harry S. *Great American Cattle Trails.* New York, Dodd, Mead, 1965.

_____. *Wild, Wooly & Wicked.* New York, C.M. Potter, 1960.

Dykstra, Robert. *The Cattle Towns.* New York, Knopf, 1968.

Faulk, Odie B. *Dodge City, the Most Western Town of All.* New York, Oxford University Press, 1977.

Foy, Eddie. *Clowning Through Life.* New York, E.P. Dutton, 1928.

Gard, Wayne. *The Great Buffalo Hunt.* New York, Knopf, 1959.

Horan, James. *Across the Cimarron.* New York, Crown Publishers, 1956.

Kansas State Historical Society. *Collections and Quarterlies.* Topeka, K.S.H.S.

Lake, Stuart N. *Wyatt Earp, Frontier Marshal.* Boston, Houghton Mifflin, 1931.

Miller, Nyle. *Great Gunfighters of the Kansas Cowtowns, 1867-1886.* Lincoln, University of Nebraska, 1967.

Myers, John M. *Doc Holliday.* Boston, Little, Brown, 1955.

O'Connor, Richard. *Bat Masterson.* Garden City, N.Y., Doubleday, 1957.

Rath, Ida E. *Early Ford County.* North Newton, Kansas, Mennonite Press, 1964.

_____. *The Rath Trail.* Wichita, McCormick-Armstrong, 1961.

Richards, Colin. *Mysterious Dave Mather.* Santa Fe, Press of the Territorian, 1968.

Rosa, Joseph. *The Gunfighter, Man or Myth?* Norman, University of Oklahoma, 1969.

Sandoz, Mari. *The Buffalo Hunters.* New York, Hastings House, 1954.

_____. *The Cattlemen.* New York, Hastings House, 1958.

Snell, Joseph. *Painted Ladies of the Cowtown Frontier.* Kansas City, Mo., Lowell Press, 1965.

Strate, David K. *Sentinel to the Cimarron.* Dodge City, Cultural Heritage Center, 1970.

Streeter, Floyd B. *Prairie Trails & Cow Towns.* New York, Devin Adair, 1963.

Tilghman, Zoe A. *Marshal of the Last Frontier; Life and Services of William M. Tilghman.* Glendale, A. H. Clark Company, 1949.

Vestal, Stanley. *Queen of Cowtowns, Dodge City.* Lincoln, University of Nebraska, 1972.

Wellman, Paul I. *The Trampling Herd.* New York, Carrick & Evans, 1939.

Wenzl, Timothy F. *Discovering Dodge City's Landmarks.* Spearville, Kansas, Spearville News, 1980.

Wheeler, Keith. *The Townsmen.* New York, Time Life, 1975.

Wright, Robert M. *Dodge City, the Cowboy Capital.* Wichita, Wichita Eagle Press, 1913.

Young, Frederic R. *Dodge City, Up Through a Century in Story and Pictures.* Dodge City, Boot Hill Museum Inc., 1972.

INDEX